GOING MY WAY?

GOING MY WAY?

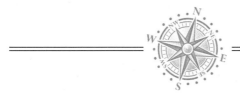

Tales of Travel

STEPHEN A. IMBEAU

Published in the United States of America by Credo House Publishers,
a division of Credo Communications LLC, Grand Rapids, Michigan
credohousepublishers.com

ISBN 978-1-62586-192-4

Cover and interior design by Sharon VanLoozenoord
Editing by Pete Ford

Printed in the United States of America
First Edition

Library of Congress
Going My Way? By Stephen A. Imbeau
LCCN 2020921343
Copy placed with the Library of Congress
US Programs, Law, and Literature Division
Cataloging in Publication Program
101 Independence Ave, SE
Washington, DC 20540-4283

Editor's Note
Stephen A. Imbeau has served as a citizen columnist for the *Morning
News* in Florence, South Carolina, since 2013. He has written at least one
column per month since then. All of them have been interesting and
informative. For the record, Stephen has permission from me and the
Morning News to publish a collection of his columns that have appeared
on the *Morning News*'s Opinion page. If there is any reason to contact
me, I can be reached at (843) 731-1728 or at *dkausler@florencenews.com*.
Regards, Don Kausler Jr. Editor: *Morning News* (Florence, SC)

CONTENTS

PREFACE

"WE STOOD in the cool breeze with sunlight streaming through clouds looking over the cliffs of Pointe du Hoc in quiet awe with tears running down our faces, three close friends." So begins one of the columns you'll find in this variegated collection that covers riveting topics in the travel category.

In early 2013, I learned the *Morning News* of my town, Florence, South Carolina, was looking for writers, creating what they called the Citizen Columnist Corps. I sent in some writing samples, was called in for interviews, and was chosen to join the team. Since then I have written over 150 articles and have enjoyed the work immensely.

My style is to tell a history, sometimes with information I don't think most people know, with some humor and personal stories along the way. My bona fides are a lifetime of world travel, personal experience running a small business, a bit of politics, and a knack for curious observation.

Whether readers are standing with my friends on the cliffs of Pointe du Hoc, discovering San Francisco, bellying up to the bar in the Wild West, or participating in some other interesting travel experience, one thing is certain: they won't be bored.

I hope you enjoy this book. Buy some for your friends. I think they will make great gifts.

Stephen A. Imbeau,
March 2021

Airplane Travel Has Its Share of Ups and Downs

Wright brothers' first flight, December 17, 1903

AIR TRAVEL has come a long way since the Wright brothers, both bachelor mechanics and inventors from Dayton, Ohio, flew 852 feet in fifty-nine seconds at a height of about ten feet on December 17, 1903, off the dunes of Kitty Hawk, North Carolina.

Today, we fly in airplanes as if they were buses or cars. There are thousands of aircraft manufacturers around the world and tens of thousands of aircraft in service.

Americans are probably most aware of the Boeing Company, named for one of its engineer founders, William Boeing. It originated in 1916 in Seattle, moved its headquarters to Chicago in 2001 after absorbing the McDonnell Douglas Aircraft Company, and now has a large plant just north of Charleston, South Carolina. The Boeing Company has produced many thousands of commercial aircraft and currently produces the 737, 747, 767, 777, and 787; Boeing also has a large space and military division.

In 1928, the City of Florence purchased about three hundred acres to the east of town to develop an airfield. During World War II, the US government bought up about another 1,400 acres around the small airfield for flight training and a POW camp. After the war, the government donated it all back to the city, calling it Gilbert Field; the city divided the eventual modern airport with the county.

In 1999, the Florence airport was placed under the Florence Regional Airport District (the City of Florence and the counties of Florence, Dillon, and Marion) and the airport is now named the Florence Regional Airport. American Airlines has five flights a day to Charlotte, from which you can reach the world.

Air travel became much more expensive and hassling after the September 11 bombings in New York and DC. There was a time when you could take a flight without reservation, pay in cash, and carry no luggage. Now you have to take off your shoes and metal objects, prove who you are, and pass through metal scanners. Even charter flights are more difficult and more expensive because of insurance costs.

Flying gets to be routine and boring, but you can read books telling you how to survive air travel. They will tell you about adjusting your sleep schedule, what to eat or drink, what kind of pillows to use, how to use eyeshades, to bring your own earphones, and how to entertain yourself.

I have narcolepsy (a sleeping illness); all I do is put my head on my shoulder, shut my eyes, and I'm usually asleep before the plane leaves the runway, often not awakening until landing. There was a time when the same plane would fly to another city without asking connecting passengers to disembark; I was on one of those once and was supposed to get off for another flight, but instead, I slept right on through until

the plane landed at its final stop. You can imagine my surprise when I did not recognize the airport and then my consternation when I saw the name of the airport; fortunately, the airline was kind and returned me to my original itinerary without extra charge.

But flying can still be fun. Once I flew to Europe with some wealthy friends; they were in first class (I never fly first class, since I just sleep). When I awoke, I decided to have some fun and enlisted a stewardess in my prank. She gave me several white towels and a travel shoe shine kit, and I went to first class and bowed and then knelt in front of my friends and began to shine their shoes. The surrounding passengers laughed and clapped and one asked me to shine his shoes, but I said, "Sorry, sir, but I only work for these gentlemen."

I have responded to "Is there a doctor on board?" calls four times and once was given a gold-headed golf putter.

Muskoka: A Brief History of the Beautiful Land

MUSKOKA IS A LAND AREA of about 2,500 square miles just east of the Georgian Bay of Lake Huron and the premier vacationland of Canada. More than 1,600 lakes and magnificent granite and Precambrian shield rock make for a spectacular setting for a vacation or a summer "away from it all," not to mention the cooler weather from the major cities of North America.

The year-round population of about sixty thousand swells by more than a hundred thousand during the summer months. The larger area around, called Cottage Country, has more than two million visitors per year. The beautiful people—including Steven Spielberg, Tom Hanks, Mike Weis, Martin Short, Harry Hamlin, Cindy Crawford, Goldie Hawn, and Kurt Russell—have summer cottages on one of the three major lakes that include Rousseau, Joseph, or Muskoka, along with other cottagers from all over the world.

The name comes either from the name of the lake or a First Nations Chief Yellowhead (Mesqua Ukie). The Chief died in fine government housing in Orillia at age 85. The Ojibwa, Algonquin, and Huron tribes lived in the area until the first Europeans came in about 1840 to trap beaver. Later, Irish and German immigrants came to log the plentiful timber stands. The first railroad was built to Gravenhurst in 1875 from Lake Simcoe and Toronto. Roads also came, but they were built of solid rock and logs to keep them stable in the summer's deep mud and were barely passable.

The English Free Grants and Homestead Act of 1868 changed everything as the English government encouraged folks to come north from Lake Simcoe to farm and hunt, but farming was not realistic on rocks. The development of a steamship line on Lake Muskoka in 1866 by Alexander Cockburn also contributed to change. By 1871, the steamships could transverse all three lakes with the opening of the Port Carling locks. The early steamships are still fondly remembered: the Seguin and the Sagamo, now restored or rebuilt, still sail today.

Hamer Bay

John Campbell and James Bain brought the first tourists to Muskoka in 1860. The first grand hotel, the Rousseau House, was built in 1870, followed by the Royal Muskoka, the Windermere, and the Beaumaris. Finally, paved roads came in the 1930s and the area had a spike of growth and tourism. By the 1950s, the steamboats were gone, replaced by automobiles. Tourism and overnight lodging became the main industry of the area. After

World War II, the middle class came, bringing cars, cottages, and fiberglass boats all over the Muskoka Lakes shorelines. Highway 400 is now a major four-to-six lane highway all the way from Toronto to Sudbury.

We are among that number with a small cottage on a small piece of stunning shoreline on Lake Joseph. Our area was developed by a professor from the University of Michigan who purchased about thirty acres from the Dixon family land grant bequeathed by Queen Victoria. Around 1930, he built a year-round greenhouse, a water tower, and experimental gardens, where we are told he developed roses and worked with tomatoes.

Later, a family in the timber business from West Virginia developed a private summer fishing camp on about thirteen acres for their friends and family. Because of health and fire concerns, the kitchen and staff house and the entertainment and sleeping house were separated by about a hundred yards, serviced by a small incline railroad, parts of which persist

An old-style Lake Joseph cottage

today. The property went dormant for about ten years and then was purchased in about 1968 and divided between the Burkes and family friends, who developed separate family compounds. The Imbeaus purchased their seven acres from the Burkes in 1997 and have loved it ever since. We have been pleased and sort of proud that so many friends have come to visit.

The grand era is over, but the grandeur of Muskoka, the Beautiful Land, remains forever.

Hear Them Tracks a-Hummin':
A Railroad History

Swiss Train to Mount Eiger, model

MUCH OF THE WORLD still moves by train—both people and goods.

The idea of using rails for transport goes way back. Ancient Greeks used carts moved by rail with animal or human power.

The modern era of railroads and trains was not possible until the invention of the steam engine by the Englishman James Watts. But the Watts system was not practical for trains until the development of high-pressure steam engines, which was adapted for practical train locomotive use in 1811 by John Blenkinsop. By 1825, steam engine locomotives were made available and safe for public transport.

Even though England tried to keep its steam engine technology at home to protect its textile industry, the steam engine soon spread throughout the world leading to what we call the Industrial Revolution. Train service came to the United States in about 1828, and by 1830 several famous steam engine locomotives were in service such as "Tom Thumb," developed by Peter Cooper.

South Carolina was an early developer of extensive rail service. The Civil War proved both the usefulness and fragility of rail lines. Despite the Civil War, the United States was able to complete transcontinental rail service by 1869, a major accomplishment and key to the development of the Western United States. Today, the United States has about 233,000

The German Technology Museum, Berlin

miles of rails, 62 percent of which are dedicated to freight.

Electricity became generally available by 1838 and was used to power train engines. By the 1890s, most major cities had developed electric rail systems for public transport.

In the 1940s and 1950s, locomotive power was gradually switched to diesel engines and the era of the steam engine locomotive was over. But nostalgia for steam locomotives persists. People love to listen to recordings of the steam whistles and sounds of their start-up and shutdown.

Amusement parks still use steam locomotives. Model railroaders delight in the steam engines on their layouts. I have filled a room at home with a model railroad track and about half of my engines are models of old steam engine locomotives.

Much of the early development of Florence was due to railroads. General W.W. Harllee of the Wilmington and Manchester railroad named the city after his daughter. The city became the hub of the Wilmington and Man-

Model trains

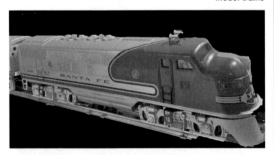

chester, the Northeastern, and the Cheraw and Darlington railroads.

And, of course, much of the old Florence downtown was built to service the railroad folks with hotels, restaurants, entertainment, dry goods stores, services, and housing. Throughout the years, the railroad influence on Florence has waned, but McLeod Hospital has restored some of the old railroad buildings for office space and the Amtrak passenger station. Amtrak stops in Florence on its north-south East Coast routes. The Florence rail switchyards are important in the modern CSX railroad system.

I rarely ride trains in the United States, but recently have found the Amtrak system a convenient way to ride along the coast, particularly since the lines coming to Florence provide night-time trips. Since I have narcolepsy, I just sit down, put my head back, and wake up at my destination. I often make day trips, leaving Florence at about 11 p.m., going to meetings all day, and then returning the same day, getting back to Florence sometime after midnight.

Rarely have I seen passengers with coats and ties, so I wear khakis, carrying other clothes in a small bag, or wear a jacket to conceal what I am wearing. In Europe, I have traveled all around by train. Europeans use trains like we use busses and cars. Europe has many more rail routes than the United States and designs its rail system for passengers, while ours is predominately designed for freight. And the European food on trains is particularly good. In modern Europe, you can carry a credit card

or cash and quickly purchase tickets to almost anywhere at a computer kiosk.

I have had some amusing experiences on European trains. Once, I was touring with some friends, and we decided to take a day trip to Mount Eiger. Of course, we took a train, but we forgot that the cars are labeled on the outside according to destination. Well, we asked some students on the station ramp if "this" was the correct train to Grindelwald, and they said "yes," but we got on a coach car labeled "Milano," which of course is in northern Italy. Luckily, I was able to talk the Italian station master at the border into letting us all onto a return train that took us back to Grindelwald without added expense. But, shucks, we had a special, unexpected trip through the Alps to Italy and only spent about two extra hours, and it was all for free.

Also on the same trip, awakening from one of my inevitable naps, I was impressed with the majestic beauty of the Swiss Alps, and we seemed so alone and away from civilization, that I just blurted out loud "Isn't this amazing beauty? Think how far we are from highways, fast cars, and busy people. Let's enjoy this beauty and solitude." Well, the words were barely out of my mouth when the train came around a curve out of a tunnel, and right in front and over top of us was a huge, superhighway system busy with cars! You can imagine how my friends made fun of me.

I later found a model train exactly like the one we were riding with the "Milano" markings on the car, and I bought it for my collection. I put that train in a glass case and it still sits in our home.

Many friends have taken the Canadian National Railroad route from Montreal to Vancouver. The scenery is fantastic, and you can buy seats in glass-domed cars to better enjoy the view.

The CN built major hotels along the route, but now these hotels are going more and more into private ownership (the Fairmont chain has taken over many of them). Probably the most famous of these old railroad grand hotels is at Lake Louise in Banff National Park, Alberta.

Let's ride the rails.

We Love Automobiles, Too

Similar to my old '55 Chevy. I loved that car!

I HAD ARRIVED, and I was only 18 or 19 years old, a junior in college.

I had just finished fixing up a 1955 Chevy four-door sedan, and it was, oh, so fine: dark blue paint job, magnesium wheels, a roll bar, Moog suspension, powerful 327 engine (not its original), a special BorgWarner transmission, and new leather seats. What a machine.

It was all paid for by my Fuller Brush and summer Longview Fibre jobs. And about twelve weeks later, it was stolen, found abandoned with a "blown" engine.

I was both devastated and uninsured, and then I made my first serious financial error: I sold it "as is," not knowing how valuable a well-appointed 1955 Chevy would become over the years, even without an engine. Oh, well.

Cars are an important part of Americana, and even more so the Classic Cars. I know several people who restore Classic Cars at home or in commercial garages.

Believe it or not, the first car was built in China in 1672 by a Jesuit priest, Ferdinand Verbiest as a steam-powered toy (the Society of Jesus was founded to counter Luther's influence, and amazingly the Jesuits went energetically all around the world).

Steam-powered cars eventually found their way to England by 1784. The first auto patent in the United States was issued in 1789 to Oliver Evans. Curiously, in 1865, the UK passed the Locomotive Act that required all cars to have an advance man running ahead with a red flag and blowing a horn, so much were the early cars abhorred. The law was enforced until 1896.

The first real car with protected, inside seating, was not produced until 1873 by Frenchman Amedee Bolee, although the American Methodist pastor, J.W. Carhart, had produced a similar vehicle in Wisconsin in 1871 (I'm not sure about this attraction between clergy and the auto; perhaps the need to move around).

Leave it to the Americans to invent auto racing. The first race was held between Green Bay, Wisconsin, and Madison, Wisconsin, with a purse of $10,000. The race took 33 hours and 27 minutes to travel 201 miles at 6 mph!

Beginning in the mid-1880s, various inventors started to look for propulsion systems besides steam, working with gasoline internal combustion, four-stroke engines, batteries, and even hydrogen fuel cells. By 1931, internal combustion engines, whether using gasoline or diesel fuel, predominated. They were made much more efficient during World War I.

Two German families, Benz and Daimler, independently, started to manufacture cars in the late 1880s in Mannheim and Stuttgart, respectively. A Frenchman, Louis Renault, began producing cars at about the same time.

Internal combustion engines started becoming more prevalent in England by 1895 and in North America by 1896. Of course, now internal combustion engines predominate, but once again we are looking toward electric cars for environmental reasons.

The first real internal combustion engine cars were produced in the United States by the Duryea brothers, beginning in 1893, but they were outgunned by the Olds Brothers, who began mass-producing cars (the Oldsmobile) in 1901, soon followed by Thomas Jeffery, who was selling even more Ramblers, followed shortly by the Cadillac, the Ford, and the Winton.

Multiple improvements came along in quick succession, including starters, lighting, the steering wheel, overhead engine valves, camshafts, suspension systems, hydraulic brakes, and transmissions. Unfortunately, mechanical durability was poor, the roads were terrible, and lodging and food were even worse.

Auto travel was a novelty for the rich and careless. But even so, during this era, the New York to Paris race was inaugurated, and the Model T Ford became famous and affordable. Preston Tucker worked tirelessly gaining multiple patents to improve gas mileage and safety in affordable cars but could not break through the marketing clout of the Big Three automakers (Ford, Chevy, and Chrysler) in combination with Big Oil (Standard Oil/Exxon), and he only sold fifty vehicles, putting himself out of business.

Once American manufacturing power was free of World War II, American-made cars became more artful, sleek, powerful, luxurious, and desirable. They were marketed and sold all around the world.

Even though we call American cars from the 1930s vintage, it is cars from the 1950s that are mostly collected today. But then in the 1960s, European and Japanese manufacturers

Stock car racers

started to successfully market their cars in the United States, mostly stressing manufacturing quality, style, and cost.

A classic 1928 Buick

American automakers did not respond quickly enough, particularly in manufacturing quality, and the Germans made huge inroads into both the high-end market (Mercedes/Porsche) and the low-end market (Volkswagen) along with the Japanese and now also Korean and Chinese, all with both high-end and low-end, popular offerings.

Florence, of course, reflects the rest of the United States. We have almost any car represented right here or nearby. Many of our local car dealers are important members of our community and are woven into the fabric of Florence leadership. There are an astonishing number of auto dealers in Florence, new and used, up to about a hundred, and some people say a few more, according to the listing criteria.

And our region has even more. The South was the home of moonshine, with or without Prohibition, and fast cars to deliver the brew, designed to outrun and outmaneuver the Revenuer or the Feds. Now we legally race these stock cars with an organization called NASCAR, right here in Darlington.

Americans are still in love with the automobile. The auto infrastructure is a major part of government responsibility, given that there are now more than 254 million passenger cars registered in the United States. The roads, motels, and restaurants are excellent now, too.

Buy a new car today. Let's go . . .

A Pointe du Hoc Tribute:
We Remember June 6, 1944

Pointe du Hoc bunker

WE STOOD in the cool breeze with sunlight streaming through clouds looking over the cliffs of Pointe du Hoc in quiet awe with tears running down our faces, three close friends.

Pointe du Hoc is the highest point between Utah and Omaha beaches. It was the site of so much pain and suffering and bloodshed in the spring of 1944 as the United States and Allies invaded the German Empire thru France. Now it looked so calm and yet somehow grim. The early spring grass was brown-green and scruffy, and old pillboxes and fortifications marched along the cliff edge. Thick Normandy hedgerows loomed just yards behind us. Seagulls swooped and called from above. All was otherwise quiet, now.

Bomb craters, some from ten to thirty feet deep and across, were spaced along the landscape behind us and to each side as the cliffs ran parallel down the beach, cliffs that loomed over the narrow beach one hundred feet below. Most craters were now covered over with some grass, but some had bushes, flowering yellow, growing up from their sides.

The number of craters was astonishing, and yet the German fortifications were often as if they were just built yesterday, in unexpectedly good shape as a kind of weird testimony to German engineering excellence. The gun encasements were large, with room for eight to twelve soldiers and foodstuffs and bed space even with hallways cut below the soil. The cement was cast about sixteen to twenty inches thick with heavy rebar enforcement.

Working together, the French and the Americans have maintained the Pointe du Hoc site with care and respect, continued after 1979 by the American Battle Monuments Commission. Paths are carefully cut to protect the history. Monuments are tasteful and carefully placed.

The stone needle near the cliff edge at the pointe's peak is a place of reflection and meditation and even worship, as is the American Cemetery overlooking Omaha Beach a few miles away—the final resting place for many of these men.

Democracy *did* prevail at the Pointe. Despite incredible hardship, blood, and death, the Rangers' heroism prevailed. The advance held and the formidable German defenses were eventually breached. But at such a cost.

On June 6, 1944, approximately 230 US Rangers headed up the cliffs on rope ladders that were shot up the cliffs as projectiles with grappling hooks to hold to the top. But only ninety survived the first two days, even

Pointe du Hoc

though many more made the cliff top, and some of those survivors were also dead after the next several days. Some of the slain soldiers are featured along the path nearby in pictures and brief bios. All of their names are listed in a nearby museum/shrine.

The assault of Pointe du Hoc was, of course, part of the D-Day invasion of continental Europe at the Normandy Beaches. The Allies had driven the German Army out of North Africa and were moving up the Italian peninsula. Now it was time to march on to Berlin, the German capital.

Operation Overlord, it was called; twenty-four thousand troops landed the first day with seven thousand ships, including warships, landing craft, and supply ships. Eventually, during the next three weeks, 875,000 troops landed in Normandy or came in overhead as airborne, including South Carolina's own Senator John Drummond. He survived his P-47 Thunderbolt crash near the Village of Gieville, where a monument stands today in his honor.

Still, it took the invasion force until the middle of July to move into Caen. On June 6, 1944, that first invasion day, four thousand Americans died and another six thousand were wounded. In legend and reality, it became "The Longest Day."

President Reagan spoke at the Fortieth Anniversary Memorial of D-Day at the Normandy American Cemetery, the memorial near Omaha Beach, and Pointe du Hoc. His words at the Pointe were soaring and elegant:

"These are the boys of Pointe du Hoc.

These are the men who took the cliffs.

These are the champions who helped free a continent.

These are the heroes who helped end a war."

The President concluded his remarks, "Strengthened by their courage, heartened by their valor, and borne by their memory, let us continue to stand for the ideals for which they lived and died."

Amen.

Going My Way? Hitchhiking

When the mist rolls in on Highway One / Like a curtain to the day / A thousand silhouettes hold out their thumbs / And I see them and I say / You are my children / My sweet children / I am your poet.

—Joan Baez, "The Hitchhikers' Song," Vanguard Records, 1971

I STARTED COLLEGE at age 16 and hitchhiked until my early 20s, usually along the West Coast, as in the Joan Baez song, or around some big cities such as Los Angeles, Burbank, and the San Francisco Bay area.

My longest hitchhiking trip was from Oakland to Lake Tahoe, approximately two hundred miles. A few years later, I also did some hitchhiking outside the United States. As the song implies, hitchhiking was fun in those days; I often met interesting people. We were always safe.

Once, involved in a college prank, I was taken blindfolded up to the top of Mount Tamalpais, across the Golden Gate Bridge from San Francisco, and let out, alone, with no money and no ID, just my gym clothes.

At first, it was sort of neat, since it was still daylight, and I was on the edge of an abandoned Nike missile camp at 2,400 feet above sea level. I climbed the fence and looked all around the unguarded base, including empty launch sites, radars, abandoned housing, and old machinery.

But then, as the sun went down, I had no way to get home. I rode a bicycle down the mountain and left it at the front door of the local police station, then started on foot past San Quentin Prison. When I rang the buzzer on the guard station fence gate, they just yelled at me and told me to go away. I then walked across the San Raphael Bridge. Well, it's illegal to walk or hitchhike across a state bridge. Roughly halfway across the bridge, I was stopped by the California Highway Patrol (what you all would call the CHIPs), and they asked what I was doing; it was about 4 a.m.

I said, "I'm trying to get home. How about a ride?"

They said, "Can you prove who you are?"

I said, "No, but my last name is written on the backs of my tennis shoes."

The two officers said, "Get in."

Along the way, I told them what happened

Mount Tamalpais

and asked them to rescue the bike back in Sausalito, telling them where I had liberated it. But at the Richmond end of the bridge, they stopped.

I said, "Hey, how about taking me all the way home? I'll get some money and pay you."

They said, "Sorry, son, this is the end of the line and our territory."

By now it was 5 a.m., so I slept on a park bench for a couple of hours, then managed to hitchhike back to Berkeley. The elapsed time back home from the mountaintop was twenty-four hours (forty miles).

It would be rare now to even consider my Tamalpais escapade or the other hikes. Super-highways, traffic laws, the ease of air travel, a richer economy, internet ride-sharing, and cruel people have basically done away with hitchhiking. Most folks are now either afraid to be a hitchhiker or to pick up a hitchhiker.

My friend Mike from Ohio still picks up some hitchhikers and either provides them a decent meal or a word about the Christian Gospel.

With the advent of the automobile and highways, hitchhiking became a popular mode of travel, both safe and acceptable, mostly for the young, the poor or homeless, or the adventuresome. It grew by leaps and bounds during the Great Depression, as you might expect.

Most often, the hitchhiker sign is to walk along the side of the road in the direction of traffic with your arm out and the thumb up (in Africa, the palm is out; in Australia, the index finger is out).

Hitchhiking is still legal almost everywhere, but not on toll roads or main highways such as our Interstates or Europe's Autobahns.

And despite our fears, hitchhiking is still mostly safe. My old friends at the California Highway Patrol did a study of hitchhiking and found that it is indeed safe, and physical abuse is rare. A 1989 German study came to the same conclusion.

Some nations still accommodate hitchhikers. In Cuba, government employees in state cars are required to pick up hitchhikers. Holland and Israel provide safe roadside shelters for hitchhikers. Poland encourages hitchhiking by giving rewards to drivers picking up hitchhikers.

Hitchhiking in the United States is still legal in forty-four states. The City of Florence Code 19-8 basically proscribes hitchhiking, as does South Carolina Title 56: Section 56-6-5-3180, but I am told by very reliable but unnamed sources that these anti-hitchhiking laws seldom are enforced off the Interstate.

I hope you will still like me, but after about three months I exacted some revenge on my college abductors. We took the two ringleaders fifty miles east of Modesto, in the middle of nowhere near a place called Cooperstown, to what we called "the desert." But we did leave them with their drivers' license, some water, and each a twenty-dollar bill. It took them three days to get back home. We included the two travelers when we celebrated their safe return that night with pizza and beer.

Now, sing along with me and Willie Nelson: "On the road again. . . ." ("On the Road Again" by Willie Nelson, Columbia Records, 1980)

Let's Play Golf

AMERICANS LOVE GOLF. We have roughly 17,700 courses in the United States, which is half of the world's inventory of golf courses. We have several Golf Channels on television, multiple magazines, and even entire sports stores dedicated to golf, golf equipment, and golf clothes. Indeed, golf is a big business, sport, and hobby.

Presidents Dwight Eisenhower, William Clinton, and Barack Obama have added prestige to the game in our modern era. Each American generation since the early 1900s has had its golf idol(s), such as Bobby Jones, Harry Cooper, Ben Hogan, Sam Sneed, Arnold Palmer, Jack Nicklaus, Lee Trevino, Tom Watson, Greg Norman, Phil Mickelson, and Tiger Woods, to name only a few.

But we Americans did not invent or originate golf. Golf, or something very similar, was played by the ancient Romans and by the Chinese in the late Middle Ages, and in the fifteenth century in Scotland it finally developed as the sport we now recognize. Golf became

St. Andrews in Scotland

so popular that King James II of England and Scotland wrote an executive order forbidding his military (particularly the officers) from playing golf, fearing it would detract from their time at archery.

The first modern-style golf course was built in 1574 as the St. Andrews Golf Club (now the "Old Course") in Fife, Scotland. The first set of standard rules was developed in 1744, and the first official golf tournament was played in 1860 at the Prestwick Golf Club in Ayrshire, Scotland. The United States Golf Association was formed in 1894, and the Professional Golf Association in 1916. The United States now has at least 13 national championship tournaments each year.

Golf came to South Carolina in the early 1900s. Probably the oldest formal course in South Carolina was developed as the Aiken Golf Club in 1912. South Carolina now has more than 360 courses, including the famous Harbor Town Golf Club on Hilton Head Island and the Ocean Course at the Kiawah Golf Resort. Myrtle Beach has more than seventy courses and has become a major golf destination.

Florence now has approximately twenty courses in the area, and it is also an important destination for golf tourism. Incredibly, the economic impact on our area from golf tourism is at least $3 million per year without considering the multiplier effect. Several quality golfers live in our area, including Tommy Gainey, Paul Brown, Billy Hoylen, Mark Gaynor, John Orr, Buddy Baker, Billy Womack, Rick Beasley, the Jones boys, Gregg Jones, Tim Crouch, David Stone, Paul T. Davis, McCuen Elmore, Richard Warren, Allen McCall, Brian Falcone, Greg Raines, Jay Saleeby, Michael Thigpen, Brice Elvington, Keith Buckhouse, Tom Kasler, and Rocky Pearce, to name a few.

We play host to a PGA qualifying tournament at the Florence Country Club, and several of our major local institutions have tournaments each year. A few of my friends play golf each weekend. They bet roughly 50 cents per hole, because they can't afford much more, but they have a great time.

Unfortunately, I can't play golf, since my legs significantly differ in length, but I can tell you how to play and I can putt well. I was a professional golf caddy from 1964 to 1967 and at my peak made approximately $150 on a weekend day. I loved my time on the links in beautiful weather at the Sequoyah Country Club in Oakland, California. Ironically, I didn't like caddying for doctors, because they didn't tip very well and took too long to play a round.

But I made many friends among the members and traveling pros. I never will forget Bill Dailey of Dailey Chevrolet and a founding partner of the Oakland Raiders football team. He always took an interest in what I was doing at college and gave me tips that doubled almost everybody else. Occasionally, he would bring along his first coach and later partner, Al Davis. About Mr. Davis, I can say little, for as they say, "Do not speak ill of the dead" (from Greece, third century AD).

My wife Shirley has taken up golf lessons. . . . *Fore!!*

Americans Ride for Fun:
A Brief History of the Motorcycle

Riding a Ducati Monster 750 on a Michigan backroad

MY MOTORCYCLE FRIENDS: They go north, they go south, they go east (well, not very far in that direction), and they go west (lots of room out there) in their quest for space, adventure, and the feel of the highway (I hope the Scarlet Pimpernel does not mind my wordplay on his famous poem).

One of my professor friends would ride his Harley most weekends and go over to Myrtle Beach for bikers' weekends, looking tough in his leathers and all, but really not; he was just one of the professional guys who loved motorcycles.

Since World War II, motorcycles have been popular recreation in America, while in Europe they are still mostly used for specific transport. I recently drove a rented car through and around Paris; I can attest to the volume of motorcycles and motor scooters, and what a pest they can be, ignoring all traffic laws and etiquette, knowing they have the tacit right-of-way, except for stoplights. A cute story: one Parisian motorcyclist thought I had come too close to him and started to kick my right, front fender; no damage done.

As you might expect, the motorcycle grew out of the bicycle in the mid-1860s in Europe as various folks fitted bicycles with equal-sized back and front wheels and some sort of engine: electric, steam, or gasoline (called petrol by the Europeans).

It probably is a tie between the Germans, French, and English who came out with the first motorcycle. The gasoline engine obviously prevailed. The German company Hildebrand and Wolfmuller came out with the first commercial production product in 1894, called for the first time a motorcycle—"motorrad." E.J. Pennington started early production in England about the same time, also using the term "motor cycle."

The first American producer was Charles Metz in 1898 in Waltham, Massachusetts. Back in Germany, the Daimler family got into motorcycle production but later became much more famous for Porsche and Mercedes cars.

Mass production of motorcycles started in England with Royal Enfield in 1901 and

Triumph in 1902. Triumph produced five hundred units the next year, and it remains famous today.

Over in America, the Indian Motorcycle company began production in 1901 and the Harley-Davidson company in 1903. It is curious indeed that the first police force motorcycle was first used in 1911 in Berkeley, California.

World War I made motorcycles famous and profitable. Harley-Davidson ramped up 50 percent of its production for the war. Triumph sold more than thirty thousand units to the Allies war machine, particularly the Triumph H model (550cc four-stroke engine with three-speed transmission).

By 1920, Harley-Davidson was the largest manufacturer worldwide with sixty-seven dealers around the world, but then it was overcome by DKW in Germany and later BMW.

The Indian brand went out of business in 1953. The buildup to World War II again stoked production and design improvement. American use of motorcycles became social, mixing in excitement, speed, and friendship, while Europeans were practical and in a transportation mode; the American motorcycle culture was portrayed and probably molded by the 1953 movie *The Wild One*.

Then came the Japanese. Honda was founded in 1948 and produced its first widely sold motorcycles shortly afterward. The Japanese swept the world market with style, speed, and low cost.

Cruising through Glacier National Park on a 2010 Honda Goldwing

Honda was followed in the 1950s by Suzuki, Kawasaki, and Yamaha. Suzuki was helped by hiring German and Swedish engineers.

Harley-Davidson survived the Japanese invasion partly because of its distinctive style and partly because of American patriotism.

Motorcycles have all become bigger and more powerful and now even diesel-powered; 800cc engines are not uncommon.

Harley-Davidson has roared back, but even BMW, Triumph, and Ducati are popular and successful again.

China is now a motorcycle player in the developing world with cheaper bikes made from Honda designs and with ethanol-fueled engines.

I started with a Vespa in high school, then graduated to a 150 Honda after getting a full driver's license at age 15, then a 250 Honda, and I ended up with a 305 Scrambler. I loved the Scrambler, using it all the way through medical school, although I also had a red Volkswagen Beetle in my senior year of medical school.

I rode all over on the Scrambler, including to Mount Lassen, Knowland Park back trails, and all around San Francisco and Golden Gate Park. Once, as I rode through Golden Gate Park, a horse-mounted city policeman came galloping after me, and then a squad car joined him. Anyway, after a driver's license and bike registration check, they told me a bike identical to my Scrambler, even the color, had just been reported stolen. It turned out my cool teal-green colored bike was common, and not as unique as I thought; I did not have the stolen bike, of course, and was released to go on my way.

Remember all of the movies featuring motorcycles? Of course. This is part of Americana. I happen to be in a few frames of the documentary *Gimme Shelter*, in its shoot at Altamont Pass and the Rolling Stones concert, me as an innocent concertgoer with my Scrambler, bumping up against a motorcycle gang of a different sort.

I suppose I should regret that I have never owned a Harley-Davidson motorcycle. But those days are long gone for me.

Walk With Me … Back in Time: A Visit to Israel

COME WALK WITH ME through time so old that America seems young, so old that most records are now dust, so old that once-vibrant communities are now thirty feet underground.

Walk with me through Israel.

I recently spent three days exploring northern Israel, called Galilee, often within sight of the Lebanese and Syrian borders. Sure, I walked plenty, covered with my new, special sun hat, but unlike when I was riding a camel several months earlier in North Africa, this time I also rode by car along with boon friend and guide, the Driver.

I often was the Navigator, and even though neither of us was a native, we loved to discuss the history, the politics, the geography, and the archeology, and we even argued (debated), all with great gusto; and, of course, we both knew exactly where we were going, even if the two views differed.

And the food and wine. . . . We loved the food. One late lunch so filled us and took about

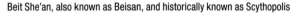

Beit She'an, also known as Beisan, and historically known as Scythopolis

Haifa panorama

ninety minutes of our time that we did not eat again for twenty-four hours, much to the dismay of his wife, who was looking forward to a nice dinner out.

We drove like Jehu along Highways 65, 72, 75, 77, 79, 85, and 89 and many more lesser roads and village streets. We had great fun going up and down the hills of Nazareth and honking at trucks and buses. Driving parallel to the Lebanon border, we could watch the radar systems of each country march along the hills, carefully watching each other. One village road on the way to Montfort Castle (featured in one of the Crusader movies) suddenly went right over the cliff ahead. We wisely got out of the car for a walk to the ruins. And even though my trusty driver and interpreter lived in nearby Haifa, we usually depended on the Waze GPS.

The cities, towns, and villages we visited included Haifa, Nazareth, Nahariya, Beitshean, Maalot, Tiberius, Acre (Akka), Safed, Zefat, and Zippori. We spent at least several hours each at the National Parks at Zippori and Beitshean. The restored 2,300-year-old synagogue at Zippori was being used by Americans celebrating a bar mitzvah. We quietly mingled with them for a while. Zippori is famous as the Maccabees family headquarters and for its stately ancient homes with astonishing mosaic floors and murals, but the hillside is now also overridden by a restored Crusader keep.

The park at Beitshean could take all day,

but I told my companion I could only walk so far in the heat, leaving it to him to climb the tell and report back. In addition to being about seven thousand years old as a city, it was the death place of King Saul and later an important local Roman capital. The Roman ruins are now the main feature, and they are still amazing. They feature more mosaics, pagan temples, well-laid-out streets (even with cart ruts), a political/market place (forum), a huge amphitheater, and a great bathhouse with running water, no less, both cold and hot. That is a testimony to the power, wealth, and majesty of the old Roman Empire, mostly forgotten by us.

The Sea of Galilee (Lake Tiberius) was beautiful and surprisingly small, about twenty miles long and, at its deepest, approximately 160 feet deep. We drove along the western half, down to the exit of the Jordan River, which is only about thirty feet wide, to later almost disappear, as the river is used for irrigation on its way south to the Dead Sea.

St. Helena (Emperor Constantine's mother) and others spent their money in Israel placing and building Catholic churches during the fourth century, saying they mark the spot of some important New or Old Testament event or site. (We now say, "Well, maybe somewhere nearby.")

And so, along Lake Tiberius we visited the Church of the Multiplication and the Church of the Beatitudes; in Nazareth, the Basilica of the Annunciation (of Angel Gabriel to Mary, that is, near Mary's Well) at the site of Mary's birthplace and her later home with Joseph, Jesus, and his siblings; and the site of Elijah's cave in Haifa (although his Mount Horeb cave is roughly three hundred miles further south), the Stella Maris Carmelite Monastery.

Each church was remarkable, although several through war, fire, or earthquake have been destroyed and then restored. The appreciation for fine detail and artwork in the ancient Catholic churches always astounds me. The Basilica of the Annunciation is remarkable for its Roman Catholic art from around the world.

Maalot is fascinating. On the one hand, it is the home of several high-tech businesses out in the hills of Galilee. And maybe because of "this" it is also the home of fascinating art. Each year the town gives twelve to twenty huge blocks of stone to interested sculptors who then prepare their piece for a sculpture judging called the "Stone in Galilee Symposium." The two best are picked as winners, and those pieces are added to the city's collection placed all around town, on street corners, in parks, in storefronts, and in front yards, all making for a great drive around town.

Our base city, Haifa, is a vibrant, majestic city build around and over Mount Carmel of ancient fame. Construction is everywhere as businesses and populations grow side by side. The people are friendly as diverse cultures mix in well since the city has been in turn Phoenician, Persian, Arab, Crusader, German, and Jewish. The Bahai came here from Iran at least fifty years before the State of Israel to establish a library and shrine within a magnificent garden flowing from mountain top to harbor.

Restaurants are everywhere, even tastefully placed along the magnificent beaches where they are famous for their seafood. We once visited the quaint Bay Club Hotel along the waterfront for evening wine. Unusual for a

major university, but Haifa University moves along the mountain top in a sprawling campus. The port has been important from Roman times; we often saw twenty to thirty ships offshore, waiting for a birth or for the container cranes.

We even had time for a modern Jewish wedding, replete with ceremony, traditional Hebrew music and dancing, great food, and American/English rock and roll and blues. The wonderful event in the lives of the couple, our hosts, and their friends lasted five hours. And then it was time to bid farewell to the Navigator, Alex, and his wife, Aggie, whose tasteful home has a magnificent view of the city and sea.

Ancient footpaths, yes, but also running eagerly into the future, vibrant with life, vision, and innovation: modern Israel.

Cruise On By

I WAS FIRMLY determined to never go on a cruise; all my life, determined. I am a creature of the land.

I like to explore, pursue city side streets, and dive down rabbit holes. I love the smell of earth, of grass and flowers, of cities and towns. And I like to watch people all around, as in a market square, or observe the macroeconomy. But the ocean? No.

After all, the water is over my head with no nearby bank; there is no end to the sea. And a ship? No streets to explore, no lanes, no inns,

Windstar Star Legend —by Shirley Imbeau

no gardens or meadows or mountains. What do you do on board? Watch the water go by?

So . . . imagine my surprise finding myself boarding a small ship, the Windstar Star Legend, in Vancouver, British Columbia, for a ten-day tour down the West Coast to San Diego with about 210 happy folks. Blame my wife, married now for forty years, plus her upcoming milestone birthday and . . . some dear friends.

They must have drugged me, for there I was in a foreign country getting ready to board a machine for a boring trip south, or so I thought. Not that I mind boring machines, as I fly all the time, but plane trips are hours, not days, and I sleep.

But, you know, I liked the cruise, time at sea notwithstanding. An obvious plus for me was that the Windstar Fleet emphasized the destinations, not the cruise itself.

The Windstar Star Legend is 443 feet of small ship elegance carrying 212 passengers and 153 crew with 106 staterooms for guests, all with ocean views. Six decks are available to the passengers with multiple restaurants, a small pool and swimming platform, several reception and entrainment lounges, and a mini theatre.

The Star Legend was German-built in 1991 as the Royal Viking Queen, then the Queen Odyssey, and then the Seabourn Legend. She entered the Windstar Fleet in 2015 as the Star Legend. She is featured in the 1997 film *Speed 2: Cruise Control*.

Typically, she sails the summer in the Alaska routes, then to the Caribbean and the

Mediterranean. We took her along the West Coast of North America from Vancouver to San Diego as she was en route to Italy via the Panama Canal for upfits to include a major enlargement, adding to the mid-section about a hundred more staterooms. A close friend from New York was soon to board her for the Panama Canal passage and Caribbean tour, I found out a couple of weeks later.

Carrying passengers on long voyages is a modern phenomenon. The Greeks, the Phoenicians, and the Vikings have been sailing the seas for millennia, but for trade, exploration, and conquest, not for pleasure; and usually no passengers were allowed who were not either sailors, warriors, scientists, or priests.

The first paying passengers climbed aboard an ocean-bound ship in 1818 for transit from England to the United States in comfort. The English led the way with, at first, the P and O Line running excursions across the English Channel and to the Mediterranean. The Cunard Line, first called the British and North American Royal Mail Steam Packet Company, next offered passenger service in high style across the Atlantic beginning in 1840 with the sailing of the Britannia, from Liverpool to New York; fresh milk and beef were provided by cows on board.

By 1844, entertainment was added. *Innocents Abroad*, a novel by Mark Twain (Samuel Clemens, American Publishing Co, 1869), charts his six-month trip, including a three-month tour of Continental Europe, on "The Quaker City." The book was a smashing success, his biggest seller ever, even with later, more famous novels.

The social classes then were strictly divided shipboard; the rich atop and the average below in steerage, often having to provide their own food and help run the ship.

By 1910, Germany and Ireland began building huge passenger liners, in particular, the Olympic and the Titanic. The Germans began cruises as early as 1910. The new ships had ele-

gant staterooms and dining rooms for the rich with ballrooms, swimming pools, and bowling alleys. Unfortunately, the Titanic sank in 1912 on its maiden voyage, ruining J.P. Morgan's White Star Line, forcing its sale to Cunard.

The World Wars put a temporary end to pleasure cruising as the ships were all converted to carry troops and material. But between the wars was a bit of a cruising golden age. Most of the travel was between the United States and Europe, and it was designed for the rich emphasizing shipboard activity and fabulous foods.

Revived post-war, European trips hit a wall in the 1950s due to high ticket prices and the ease of the new airplane travel; most cruise lines collapsed.

Island Princess

But then there was a sharp reversal in fortune built around Caribbean vacations for families and average folks starting in the late 1960s, eventually expanding to include the Mediterranean, river cruises, and the Alaska shoreline. Some river cruise lines designed barges to bind down motor campers. The big ships became Fun Ships and designed shipboard activity and entertainment for the whole family. The vacation was the cruise itself, rather than the destination, except for the river cruises.

The new success of the cruise industry spawned the long-running TV show, the *Love Boat* (eleven years on ABC, from 1977 to 1987). The new industry began to build mega passenger ships holding thousands, some ships up to ten thousand people. Some ports rejected these new, huge ships, but their economic success was undeniable. The older P and O, Cunard Luxury Cruises, and Holland American Lines continue; the new lines include Princess Cruises (1965), Norwegian Line (1966), Royal Caribbean (1968), Carnival Cruises (1972), Windstar Cruises (1984), Disney Cruises (1996), Viking Cruises (1997), and Virgin Holidays Cruises (2000).

Cruise line revenues soared to approximately $40 billion per year in 2018 with decent profit margins. Problems along the way included ship overcrowding, human illness particularly due to viruses, port problems including space and depth, resistance from some port populations, fuel costs, general economic conditions, and terrorist threats.

No mega-ships for me, but the Windstar size was just right for this Little Bear. For your next cruise, consider calling your local travel agency. And, of course, there is the Internet, including the major cruise lines' proprietary web pages.

Cruise on.

We All Love the Irish

Irish farmland

WELL, AT LEAST I DO. You see, I married one, although I'm not Irish myself.

We love Irish music, with much of it famous worldwide. Do you know the songs "When You Were Sweet Sixteen," "Danny Boy," "When Irish Eyes are Smiling," "Molly Malone," and "Auld Lang Syne" (with some license since it is Scotts-Irish)?

We dance to the tunes of Irish bands and shows touring worldwide. At many hockey games, Irish music is played during intermission to build excitement and foot-stomping.

Irish migration has helped to build our nation. The Irish are now approximately 13 percent of the US population (2013 data). Nationwide, the Irish are roughly 50 percent Catholic, but the Irish Catholics predominate in the Northeast and the Midwest, while the Irish are mostly Protestant in the South. The first wave of Irish immigration was during our Colonial period, from Ulster (what we now call Northern Ireland), of about 250,000, mostly Protestants. These folks took up community along the Appalachians and South Carolina.

A huge Irish migration of approximately two million Catholics occurred during the era of our American Civil War. These Irish were both attracted to industrial jobs in our large cities in the Northeast and the Midwest and forced out of Ireland by the Potato Famine and its mismanagement/manipulation by the British government. Over time, many of these folks migrated to police work and education, but now they work across the spectrum of professions.

During the Civil War, many new Irish immigrants were paid to join or coerced into the Union Army to fight the Confederate Army. Again, in the early 1900s, there was a third large Irish migration, mostly to the large cities in the Northeast and Midwest.

The Irish themselves now live on a divided island. The Irish Republic or Irish Free State—founded slowly from 1922 to 1933, beginning, more or less, with the Dublin Rising in 1916—is mostly to the south. Great Britain still reigns in the North over Ulster, now shrunk from its original size by three counties.

Dublin is the capital of the Irish Republic, and Belfast is the chief city of British Ireland. But West Belfast remains divided by the Peace Wall, built about twenty feet high. It is continuous for roughly six miles with intermittent gates open only during daylight, to keep the peace, mostly, between the Catholic and Protestant activists.

St. Patrick returned to Ireland to evangelize and establish churches for the Catholic Church, which of course was *the only* Christian Church in the mid-400s. Surviving Viking dominance, the Catholic influence has prevailed across most of the island. Since the time of the Normans, England slowly took control of all Ireland, assuming rule since the time of James I.

In the North, during the rule of Henry VII, England built or forced a Protestant majority in its Ulster territories, reinforced during the Dictatorship of Oliver Cromwell, a Puritan. But now, even though nominally Catholic in the Irish Republic, church attendance of all sorts has plummeted, and some of the religious labels are thus traditional, although still politically potent. The US Presbyterian and Methodist Churches have important Irish/Scotts-Irish founding roots.

The Irish have a saying that brings both a smile and a tear: "We Irish do not always have troubles, but we have enough to get us through happier times."

Now, please pass me a pint . . . of Guinness . . . mate.

"Mr. Gorbachev, tear down this wall."

The Berlin Wall then

IT WAS LATE WINTER in Berlin, and although the sun was shining and the sky was a beautiful blue, we pulled our coats around us against the chill, strolling along land previously occupied by the infamous Berlin Wall.

Now it is beautiful, with open space, monuments across City Center, even pieces of the old wall as a memorial to past shame and ugliness. On some side streets toward the canal, the city has developed mini parks along the route of the old wall complex, where children somersault down the side of grassy mounds built up to the old wall's height, as gentle reminders of a torn Germany.

Embarrassed by and reeling from both the loss of World War I and severe Allied reparations, the Germans named a young, failed house painter as their Chancellor, several years into a struggling republic. Adolf Hitler aspired to be an architect, but unlike any other architect, he was inspired to be ruler of the world, too.

His soaring, mesmerizing rhetoric and his appeal to former German greatness allowed him to sweep away the republic and become dictator after a strong, although losing, electoral showing for the presidency in 1932, but in steps. First he was appointed chancellor, then he selected his Nazi Party's leaders for important government posts. He won a Reichstag vote as dictator in late 1933 and then was named Führer in 1934.

Hitler then turned to two tasks: 1) rearming Germany for the conquest of the rest of Europe, and 2) eliminating the Jews and other undesirables. A divided Europe, weary of war, stood by and watched, and some American International corporations naively, sympathetically, helped Germany, also sensing future, long-term business opportunity.

The Berlin Wall today

Hitler's march across Europe began and prevailed for many years to be stopped only by English courage (almost supplied too late), by Winston Churchill, by Germany's ill-advised invasion of Russia, and by the Japanese forcing the United States into another World War.

The Russians captured Berlin, the German capital, from the east as Germany was finally brought to heel in 1945; the rest of the Allied armies came in from the west, through France. The Russians were keen on preventing any resurgence of the Nazi Party and thus insisted on a division of the old European nations and Germany, between spheres of influence shared between Great Britain, the United States, and Russia.

Only too late did the Americans and the English realize Russia was looking ahead to its own expanded empire.

Brandenburg Gate today

So, Germany was physically divided, and since its capital, Berlin, lay entirely within the new Russian sector, the city also was divided among the winners. Over time, the differences between West Berlin and East Berlin became evident, as did the differences between West Germany and East Germany.

Prosperity, Western culture, and freedom flourished in the West but languished in the new communism of the East. East Germans began to vote with their feet, leaving the East, eventually by the millions, mostly through Berlin.

And so, in 1961, Russian First Secretary Nikita Khrushchev, with East German Chairman Walter Ulbricht, closed the border in Berlin and started a temporary wall of barbed wire, enabled by the expected acquiescence and perceived indifference of the United States. Of course, the wall was built to keep people inside the East and to prevent observance of or access to the West's success.

Over the next thirty years, the wall was extended, both in length and in depth, and improved in stages. There is an excellent model display of these Berlin Wall changes at the Miniatur Wunderland model train exhibit in Hamburg.

Later in 1961, the wall was extended and replaced with preformed concrete sections. Within another year, a 100-yard death strip was built between a second, parallel wall with guard towers. Then, in the late 1960s, the concrete was improved. Finally, in the late 1970s, the wall was heightened, strengthened to prevent auto bashing, and electronic surveillance and armaments were added.

Despite the wall, some five thousand people were able to defect, although approximately two hundred were killed in the attempt. Two famous escapes: Wolfgang Engels drove a stolen military armored vehicle across and was rescued from the death strip by West Berlin police, and Thomas Krüger flew a small plane across. Unfortunately, two escapees were killed just months before the wall was opened.

On June 12, 1987, at Brandenburg Gate in Berlin, President Reagan began the final drive to drop the Wall.

"General Secretary Gorbachev, if you seek peace, if you seek prosperity for the Soviet Union and Eastern Europe, if you seek liberalization, come here to this gate," Reagan said. "Mr. Gorbachev, open this gate. Mr Gorbachev, tear down this wall."

Western musicians also contributed to the fall of the wall with huge, open-air concerts near the wall, including David Bowie (1987), Bruce Springsteen (1988), and David Hasselhoff (1989).

By 1989, Eastern Europe began to tear away from the Soviet Union. Refugees again began pouring out of East Germany through the east bloc Soviet States, so that finally on November 9, 1989, East Germany opened the gates. The wall was torn completely away, except for the memorial sections, over the next two years or so.

Despite expectations, it was slow going to reunite Berlin. The reunification of all Germany was even slower and very expensive. But now the city is rebuilt and the old demarcation lines are hard to find.

Curiously, the old Gestapo and Stassi headquarters are now open to the public; a private museum predominates the site of Check Point Charlie, replete with actors playing the roles of the Cold War Russian and American soldiers. Old Germany is now New Germany, rebuilt with investments from all over the world, particularly from the Americans, the Japanese, the Arab States, the Chinese, and, yes, even the Russians.

Hamburg, with the help of mostly Chinese investment, is building a new $22 billion mini-city called HafenCity; strategically perched along the Elbe River, Hamburg is now the fastest-growing city in the new Germany.

Jekyll Island Memories

IT WAS 1931 and I was struggling as a young golf caddy on Jekyll Island, Georgia.

In fact, most of the members were gone and the staff at the palatial Jekyll Island Club much reduced. America was in the Great Depression, and even the rich were affected. I decided I had nothing to lose, so I started going to the back doors of the cottages around the Island Estate for help and food. (I was not allowed to go to any front doors, you see.)

Actually, you would call the cottages mansions, but the word "mansion" was unseemly to the very rich.

Luck brought me to the door of Lord Coy and Lady Angie from New York, of royal Irish and British descent. Their servants were kind to me with a bowl of hot soup and delightful crusted bread; I could not believe my good fortune, for they also offered me a small place to sleep. My quarters were, of course, downstairs and small, the room only eight feet by twelve feet and the bed only six inches longer than me; but "beggars cannot be choosers," as they say.

After several weeks, I began to look around. I had trouble taking it all in. The grand entrance with an enormous chandelier, the drawing-room with silver and china pieces placed tastefully, the dining room with a forty-foot table and so elegantly set, and the ballroom. . . . I could just imagine the waltz and the minuet I would need to learn.

And in the library, to my surprise, were the Lord and Lady themselves; I could not believe it. I bowed low and nervously spoke, offering

Jekyll Island Club Historic District

my services as a caddy to Lord Coy. He laughed and agreed, and the next day I guided him through nine holes. We remained friends for many years, me at my proper distance from such American nobility.

The Jekyll Island Club was founded in 1886 as a private club for hunting and recreation on Jekyll Island, Georgia, after being purchased for the then-handsome price of $125,000 from John Eugene du Bignon. The project was the brainstorm of Newton Finney, Mr. du Bignon's brother-in-law, the goal being to then resell the island to a group of wealthy individuals from "up north."

In fact, they sold to fifty-three families for $600 per share and then sold the whole island in 1886 to the new group called the Jekyll Island Club. Finney and du Bignon thus made a profit on both the land and the shares.

The clubhouse was completed in January 1888. The original members included some of America's most wealthy families. In fact, it has been estimated that approximately 25 percent of America's wealth has over the years been represented in Jekyll Island Club membership. Names such as Aspinwall, Howland, Ogden, Hyde, Field, Morgan, Pulitzer, and Vanderbilt were included among the founding members.

Future memberships included famous American names such as Albright, Beard, Claflin, Daniels, Kellogg, Goodyear, Gould, Hayes, Hill, Houghton, Kennedy, Lee, Macy, McCormick, Rockefeller, George, Thayer, and Whitney. Eighteen of them built elaborate mansions on the island, called cottages.

Jekyll Island played a role in an important piece of American history. The legislation written in 1910 to establish our current US Federal Reserve banking and currency system following the US banking collapse of 1907 was drafted on Jekyll Island in the cottage of US Senator Nelson Aldrich, father-in-law to John D. Rockefeller Jr. (son of J.D. Rockefeller).

The list of draftees of this legislation is impressive: A. P. Andrews (Assistant Secretary of the Treasury), Paul Warburg (Kahn and Loeb), Frank Vanderlip (National City Bank of New York), Henry Davison (J.P. Morgan), Charles Norton (First National Bank of New York), and Benjamin Strong (J.P. Morgan). They secreted themselves out of New York City at midnight using only first names, on a private train headed to Georgia. Even while on the island, they never used their last names, so the staff could not identify them.

The legislation mostly passed as drafted and is, of course, still in use today.

Lord Coy Irwin

Another historical incident on the island: in 1915, Theodore Norton Vail, president of AT&T, organized the first transcontinental phone call from the island, connecting President Wilson in Washington, DC, Alexander Graham Bell in New York City, Thomas Watson in San Francisco, and Henry Higginson in Boston.

I suppose it's also history that the 2000 movie *The Legend of Bagger Vance* (written by Jeremy Leven from the novel by Steven Pressfield, produced by Michael Novik, Jake Eberts, and Robert Redford, by Dream Works and 20th Century Fox) was filmed on the island.

A personal note: my wife, Shirley, was in Isle of Palms for breakfast one Sunday morning when in walked Robert Redford, scouting locations for this movie.

Imagine my surprise when Lord Coy's lookalike and namesake grandson turned up in Florence to be on a local hospital administration staff; and his wife's name, too, was Angie, just like the grandmother of old.

Please do not tell Shirley my true age, by the way. I never caddied for this modern Coy but became a good friend, even after they returned to Florida and Georgia.

I must admit irritation: I never got invited back to the Lord Coy cottage, even by the grandson.

But maybe finances have changed for the Duke's family. World War II ruined the island's finances, contributing to its 1942 collapse. The State of Georgia bought Jekyll Island out of bankruptcy in 1947.

The Jekyll Island Club was restored in 1985 and is now a resort hotel operated by the Northview Hotel Group, a venture capital group based in Connecticut that owns and operates several important resort hotels.

Plantation Life:
The Huntington Estates

Live Oak trees, Brookfield Gardens

FRANCIS MARION UNIVERSITY'S recent association with Hobcaw Plantations turned my thoughts to South Carolina's famous plantations.

Since I am from California, I will start not with Hobcaw but will get back to it, since Hobcaw has a fascinating history, too. I will start with the Huntington Estates and Brookgreen Gardens near Myrtle Beach.

Most of you probably don't know, but the Huntingtons are from California. Collis Huntington was one of the "Big Four" Californians who developed the Union Pacific Railroad, fulfilling President Lincoln's dream of a trans-

continental railroad, despite a raging civil war.

The "Big Four" were Collis Huntington, Leland Stanford, Charles Crocker, and Mark Hopkins. All but Hopkins came out of the "wild west days" of the California Gold Rush, emerging as successful merchants and small manufacturers in Sacramento, California. Two of them married strong-willed women of adventure.

Upon learning of the proposal by the US government to develop a transcontinental railroad, they recognized opportunity. They formed "The Associates" investment group, then the Central Pacific Railroad, and eventually the

Southern Pacific-Union Pacific Railroad. With associates and construction experts, they build the railroad east to Promontory Point, Utah, connecting with the Union Pacific line with the famous Golden Spike on May 10, 1869.

Central Pacific Railroad Logo 1869

The railroad project made them all very rich. They were imaginative as they made money off the project with miraculous stretches of miles of mountainous terrain, stock manipulations, land sale schemes, and labor negotiations, but their determination and talents were formidable and provided a very important rail link across the country for the United States.

The Four mastered management, logistics, supplies/material, shipping, commodities, and labor against great obstacles to link a nation; in fact, to forge a New Nation. The project also built significant Eastern fortunes in iron and steel, shipping, and commodities. So, the project was really very good for the economy of the whole country. Basically, the Big Four deserved their money; their success forgave all of their sins. Multiple novels, histories, and movies have come out of this project and its lore.

Leland Stanford became the governor of California and the founder of Leland Stanford Junior University. (Interesting side story here: after the death of son Leland Jr. in Europe, Harvard University lost a major donation offer from the Stanfords, as Boston would not company with unsophisticated California gold rush merchants and showed them little regard in an interview.)

Sadly, Stanford, a junior university, still lags behind the University of California-Berkeley, except in football. We educated folks don't have the athleticism of the Farm men and women down the Bay.

Mark Hopkins stayed in the railroad business; Collis Huntington stayed in the railroad business, adding shipbuilding; and Charles Crocker went into banking. In later years, the four partners built mansions in San Francisco on what is now called "Nob Hill," because in those days the four were also called the "nabobs."

Collis Huntington was sent by the partners to Washington, DC, to lobby for the nascent railroad project. He was very successful in DC, although he was ruthless and said to be unscrupulous. He managed to arrange for significant federal funding based on miles of track and toughness of terrain and magically transformed the map to both add miles and extend mountains. He convinced Congress to give wide swaths of land to his partners along the train route, usually at least a mile on each side of the route, up to twenty miles.

He also raised significant private money. Presidents Lincoln, Johnson, and Grant overlooked all of the politics, skullduggery, and "pork," as they were all determined to have the railroad built.

Samson and the Lion sculpture, Brookgreen Gardens

Fortune established, Collis Huntington went on to complete the Chesapeake and Ohio Railroad with important West Virginia coal mine extensions, and then he developed the Newport News Shipbuilding Company along with the town of the same name. The Huntingtons stayed in the East, even though they built a mansion in San Francisco. Collis Huntington's stepson Archer Huntington is the reason they are now in South Carolina.

Archer Huntington married Anna Hyatt, a sculptor. The Huntingtons visited South Carolina in 1929 and fell in love with the land. They purchased approximately nine thousand acres along the ocean in Waccamaw Neck for a winter home to escape the Connecticut chill. But Anna also saw it as a potential site for her sculptures and other American sculptors, including her sister, Harriet Mayor. By 1932, they had developed the Archer and Anna Hyatt Huntington Sculpture Garden (Brookgreen Gardens), and over time filled it with more than 1,445 works of American sculpture.

Approximately two thousand acres of the park have been placed in the National Registry of Historic Places and Landmarks. The garden is open to the public by fee and offers annual memberships. Educational programs and special exhibits are available. The garden hosts a spectacular display of art and lights each Christmas season. Some of the property also displays old rice plantation life and structures.

Huntington descendants remain or visit nearby in other Huntington land across U.S. Route 17, including Atalaya Castle. Some beachfront Huntington land is now leased to the State of South Carolina for a state park with the same name.

So, see, California has been a benefit to South Carolina.

More Plantation Life: The Hobcaw Barony

FRANCIS MARION UNIVERSITY'S recent association with Hobcaw Barony and the Belle Baruch Foundation turned my thoughts to South Carolina's famous plantations.

There are at least three Hobcaw plantations in South Carolina: "Hobcaw Barony" in the Georgetown-Myrtle Beach area, one near Kingstree in Williamsburg County, called "Little Hobcaw," and another near Charleston.

"Hobcaw" is a Native American word meaning "between the waters." The word is also used for several developments in Florida. Hobcaw Barony and Little Hobcaw were once owned by famed financier Bernard Baruch.

Baruch was born on August 19, 1870, in Camden to a Jewish physician's family. His parents were successful, and while in South Carolina his mother, Belle Wolfe Baruch, was a prominent member of the Daughters of the Confederacy, and Dr. Baruch had served as a Confederate Army surgeon.

When Bernard was eleven, his family moved to New York City. He graduated from the City College of New York. He was ecumenical, marrying Annie Griffin, an Episcopalian, smart and aggressive. And he became very rich.

Before age thirty, Baruch founded his own Wall Street brokerage after buying a seat on the New York Stock Exchange with money earned and saved from the A. A. Housman and Company brokerage. He rarely joined with others, preferring to work alone, the original "Lone Wolf of Wall Street."

By 1910, he was a prominent Wall Street financier. His early money was made in the sugar markets, including investing in Hawaii and its sugar trade. He retired from business in 1916. Much of the rest of his life was spent in government and philanthropy. He is probably the inspiration for "Daddy Warbucks" in the famous *Little Orphan Annie* (Harold Gray, Tribune Media services, 1924) comic strip series (and the play and movie *Annie* from Thomas Meehan, 1976).

Beginning at retirement, Baruch began to work with President Wilson to later also work with Presidents Roosevelt and Truman, mostly on war-related economics and then atomic energy. He worked during both World Wars to help the United States mobilize industrial war production, manage the economy during the wars, and then make the peace.

He attended the Paris Peace Conference and worked with the League of Nations, and then after the next war, he served on the United

Nations Atomic Energy Commission to present the Baruch Plan to control atomic weapons; his plan was rejected by the Soviet Union.

In 1905, Bernard came back to South Carolina in a big way. He began to buy property, eventually called the Hobcaw Barony from an earlier use of the term for some of the same land granted by English King George I in 1718 to John Lord Carteret on sixteen thousand acres near Georgetown. By 1850, the original plantations were famous for quality rice, called "Carolina Gold," produced by thousands of African-American slaves until the Civil War and thereafter as freed men and women, many of whose descendants still live and work in the local area, often still living in the old slave villages and cabins until the 1950s.

Baruch developed the property and restored many of its old buildings to develop a winter hunting retreat to which he invited many important New York and Eastern Seaboard folks, including President Roosevelt and England's Sir Winston Churchill. Several Churchill paintings grace the walls. President Roosevelt spent the month of April 1944 at Hobcaw Barony recovering from congestive heart failure; he loved the plantation so much that he credited it with saving his life.

The plantation was sold to Belle W. Baruch, Bernard's daughter, in 1955. She arranged for it to pass after her death to the Belle Baruch Foundation to be used for environmental research and education. The property was placed on the National Register of Historic Places on November 2, 1994.

Since the foundation accepted the land, the Hobcaw Barony has worked with the University of South Carolina and Clemson University to study the land and to help operate and maintain it. Other South Carolina research schools have joined in. The studies through the BWB Institute for Marine and Coastal Science concentrate on coastal ecosystems, marine biology, Native American history (the Waccamaw tribal peoples), slavery, and rice plantation management and life.

The waters of Hobcaw Barony are considered the most pristine of their type in the world. One of the important ongoing research projects is water quality and restoration, research that has potential global significance.

The Little Hobcaw on approximately four thousand acres near Kingstree was purchased in 1933 by Bernard Baruch for much the same use as Hobcaw Barony, but it was favored by him because it was closer to Camden. It became his favorite quail hunting reserve. He also entertained notables at the Kingstree plantation. Several Churchill paintings were also hung at Little Hobcaw.

The Little Hobcaw Plantation was managed for the Baruchs by members of the McGill family, who later became prominent politicians in South Carolina and real estate brokers. The plantation was sold in 1965 to James Sigmon. The property was recently placed again on the market for "only" $12 million.

(Editorial assistance and some of the history came from a Belle Baruch Foundation board member, Ben Zeigler.)

A Day of Infamy

WE STOOD ON A BARGE one evening near the Arizona Memorial as the golden sun slipped below the hills and water of Pearl Harbor to honor America's heroes of World War II tragically killed during the surprise bombing on December 7, 1941.

It was a scene of honor, a frightful memory for some people, and tragic loss, but it was cast in an important and hopeful light by glistening ranks of sailors in white, the white "bridge" over the ruins of the USS Arizona, a Marine Band, and military jets in procession overhead. Tears were in eyes all around us.

USS Arizona Memorial

Actually, the quote is ". . . a date which will live in infamy. . . ." That was taken from the next morning's speech of President Franklin Delano Roosevelt as he declared war against the Empire of Japan to a joint session of Congress.

The Japanese delivered a formal declaration of war to the U.S. Department of State only an hour after the attack began on Pearl Harbor. Interestingly, Japanese envoys were in Washington, DC, at the time to ostensibly negotiate a peace with the United States. The Axis Powers of Italy and the German Empire followed into war against the United States over the next several days.

Despite a raging war in Europe between the Allies and the Axis and in Asia between Japan and her neighbors—including a Japanese invasion of China and others—America had stayed out of direct involvement in these wars until the president's proclamation of December 8, 1941.

Japan had planned the Hawaii attack since at least that March, calling it Hawaii Operation, Operation AI, or Operation Z. Pearl Harbor was chosen since it was the headquarters of the US Pacific Fleet and because the Japanese did not consider it to be well guarded or protected. Furthermore, the harbor was narrow and shallow with airfields nearby. The Japanese did not ever intend to follow on to San Francisco or Seattle, but they thought a severe and successful attack on Hawaii would discourage America from any more thought of war, particularly against Japan.

The Japanese viewed the Americans as weak and self-absorbed; several important Japanese families had family members living in California, particularly San Francisco, as professionals, intellectuals, and thought leaders, so they assumed they knew the American culture and mood.

But, of course, they were wrong. America awoke from the attack after a 21-year slumber to make a major and decisive contribution in both the European and Asian war theaters.

Among the Japanese elites, basically only Admiral Yamamoto warned of the risks of surprising America at Pearl Harbor unless the US mainland also was attacked soon afterward.

The Japanese attacked by air out of the northwest shortly before 8 a.m., approximately thirty minutes after sunrise—after all, the logo or symbol of Japan is the Rising Sun.

We had built radars in the Hawaiian Islands over the previous 18 months or so, mostly on Oahu, Hawaii, and Kauai; the islands of Hawaii and Kauai remain important radar sites today. But the technology was new, the observers not all fully trained and the linkages fragile. Images were thought to be "noise," or birds; the commander thought for a while that the images were the secret air squadron coming to Hawaii from California that morning. Also, a mini submarine periscope was sighted as early as 3 a.m., yet no general alarm was raised.

Astonishingly, there also was an attitude of, "Hey, it's Sunday morning; time for golf, family picnics, and church services—certainly not war." But onward came the Japanese planes with deadly intent.

The Japanese force was carried by six aircraft carriers and five submarines; the carriers launched 353 aircraft (bombers, torpedo planes, gunners, reconnaissance, and support aircraft), and the subs carried one mini submarine each. Only 29 Japanese aircraft were shot down (another 74 planes were damaged), and all of the mini submarines were destroyed; the Japanese suffered 64 dead and one captured (from a mini submarine). A Japanese mini submarine was sunk as late as 6:30 that evening.

AP Photo

But the destruction for America was horrific, the only good news being that Admiral Nimitz had sent the aircraft carriers offshore over the previous two months, for random reasons. We lost four battleships (six more were damaged), three cruisers, four auxiliary ships, and one tender ship.

We were later able to raise three of the sunken battleships due to shallow water; the damaged ships were all later returned to the war theater.

The Battleship Arizona was not raised and remains a grim, spectacular memorial to that day, and it is a final resting place of many of its survivors who wished to be buried there in later years. We also lost 188 planes parked along the airfields. The human toll was even worse: 2,403 Americans were killed that day, and another 1,178 were wounded, including sailors, Marines, Navy, and Army airmen, civilian aides and officers.

American memories of horrible destruction and incredible heroism remain from that one day of infamy.

The tragedy shook America. However, we arose to arm ourselves for war and to eventually help bring peace back to the earth.

AP Photo

What's a Brexit?

WHAT'S A BREXIT? On one hand, it's easy: it's the slang term for the British exit from the European Union. But, on other hand, nobody really knows. And for sure, as of today, nobody knows how to "do it."

We four tourists were fortuitously in London at the supposed close of the British Effort to leave the European Union (EU), Brexit, in March of 2019. The United Kingdom (the UK is composed of England, Scotland, and Northern Ireland) joined the then-European Community (EC) in 1973, after the retirement of Charles de Gaulle of France, who had blocked the UK entry.

Once accomplished, there was almost immediate UK debate and argument about the EC entry action of conservative leader Edward Heath, then the British prime minister. Arguments against the UK staying in the EC/EU included general distaste for rule from Brussels or Strasbourg, fear of German dominance in EU politics, EU immigration policies, concerns about the border between the Irish Republic and Northern Ireland, and the economic problems of the Mediterranean EU countries.

After many years of political ups and downs, the UK held a general referendum on June 22–23, 2016, and voted 51.89 percent in

Parliament, London

Brexit protest

and the boundary between the Republic of Ireland and Northern Ireland (open or closed?).

In the background were also Brexit political divisions within both of the two major UK political parties (Tory and Labor) and Brexit policy differences between Scotland and England.

We witnessed the second rejection of the prime minister's reworked exit agreement deal with the EU, then the rejection of a straight-out exit from the EU without any mutual agreements, and finally the endorsement of at least a ninety-day extension of the originally legislated on March 29, 2019, the exit date. Another "deal vote" is imminent, but its timing is in doubt, as the House of Commons Speaker has ruled the new Deal cannot be like the previous one. A new vote was scheduled in June, but Prime Minister May stepped down on June 7.

Boris Johnson was elected Prime Minister on July 22, 2019, after the resignation of Theresa May. He had enough votes in Parliament to pass a Brexit Bill agreeable to the EU in Parliament on December 20, 2019, with a withdrawal date of January 31, 2020 and transitional period ending December 31, 2020.

favor of leaving the EU (American observers had predicted only a two-point spread). The Conservative Party—led by Theresa May, after David Cameron's resignation, but not always with a majority in Parliament—began to negotiate the UK withdrawal from the EU in a series of "rounds" to arrive at a final European Union Withdrawal Act that was approved by Parliament in June 2018.

The real trouble began when final details of the Exit Deal with the EU were presented in January 2019 and defeated in a lopsided British Parliament, House of Commons, vote. The prime minister survived a "no-confidence" vote. There were several sticking points: trade and commerce agreements (whose regulations would prevail: EU or UK?); financial reparations; travel and immigration; money exchange and finance; overreaching authority;

We walked or rode in the vicinity of Parliament Square and Whitehall with its many famous statues and government buildings, witnessing orderly protesters on both sides of the issue, waving flags and slogan banners. Several times we maneuvered around members of Parliament, awaiting entry to debate or vote.

Most local economists felt the UK should stay in the EU, but for sure, should certainly not leave without a "deal." All of our black cab drivers made passionate Brexit speeches; the Uber drivers kept quiet.

Important history is in the making!

My Favorite US Cities: San Francisco

ALTHOUGH BORN in Portland, Oregon, I grew up in the Bay Area of San Francisco, specifically in Oakland, educated both in Berkeley and San Francisco through the University of California system. So . . . we will start with San Francisco. Despite all of its cultural changes over the years, it remains my favorite United States city.

The prominence of San Francisco has always been predicated on its location at the mouth of a huge bay (1,600 square miles) called the San Francisco-Oakland Bay or just the Bay Area. At least five thousand years ago, in the era of biblical Job, the San Francisco Bay Area was settled by the indigenous Ohlone people, who became entrepreneurs and traders, developing customers and contacts all along the West Coast.

The Spanish were the first persistent European settlers, muscling aside the Ohlone in 1769, through Gaspar de Portola, governor of California (born in Balaguer, Spain). Over the next fifty years or so, the Spanish resisted French, English, and Russian interest, although allowing a Russian fur-trading base.

The Spanish did not develop much, more interested in Christian missionary work, common for the Spanish along the length of California, developing the San Francisco Mission de Asis (named after St. Francis, the city's namesake) now called Mission Dolores (Sorrows/Pain) after a nearby creek named for Mother Mary. A revised, magnificent Catholic Church stands at the site to this day.

San Francisco skyline

Mexico took ownership after the 1821 Revolution. In 1835, the Mexicans allowed some English to begin development along the bayside of the peninsula, which eventually attracted Americans. When the Americans learned the English were interested in all of California, they started moving west and could no longer be resisted.

A group of migrating Mormons convinced the United States to "annex" the area in 1846, as we were then defeating the Mexicans in the Mexican-American War. The Treaty of Guadalupe Hidalgo in 1848 made all of California officially part of the growing United States; US statehood came in 1850.

All has never been the same since the Gold Rush of 1848–50, which increased the population twenty-five-fold. A huge Chinese immigration along with prospectors (we now call the 49ers) from America and all around the world came to work in the goldfields, support businesses, and the succeeding railroad development.

San Francisco continues to have the second-largest Chinese population in the United

Famous Lombard Street

States, although recent mainland Chinese emigration has reduced the worldwide status of San Francisco's Chinatown. I have already written about the history of the railroads, the Big Four, and the development of San Francisco (see "Plantation Life: The Huntington Estates"). Other famous businesses springing up during the Gold Rush include Levi Strauss, Wells Fargo Bank (see "Galloping to Legend," January 15, 2019, *Morning News-SCNow*), and Ghirardelli chocolates.

Surviving cholera, crime, corruption, and the Civil War, San Francisco "really" grew in the 1860s. A quaint, popular reminder of those days remains: Andrew Smith Hallidie's "cable cars."

My medical school was founded in 1864 by a wealthy local surgeon, Hugh Toland, MD. The city became a banking and trade center, rebuilt bigger and better with the foresight of developer-planner Daniel Burnham and banker Amadeo Giannini (Bank of Italy, now Bank of America) after the destructive earthquake and fire of 1906.

Two of my favorite places came out of that era: Golden Gate Park and Fisherman's Wharf.

The city continued to grow during the world wars as a huge maritime shipping and construction port. A population shift occurred

as people came from the Dust Bowl and the Deep South to work in the Henry Kaiser Industry shipyards building Liberty ships (completing one ship a day at production peak). Subsequent redevelopment led to more cultural dislocation.

Enter my era of the 1960s and 1970s. Because of the arts, literature (the city had long been a writers' haven), and music, a United States counterculture arose, but the new culture also revived United States-based rock 'n' roll music (see "Music Forever," August 29, 2019, *Morning News-SCNow*) accompanied by a large influx of gay people, starting after the World War and in large part responsible for the United States gay liberation movement.

In the 1980s, HIV-AIDS wreaked havoc across the city, although the virus originated in Africa, coming west through Quebec City; but the new epidemic also led to important AIDS treatment science and prevention programs.

Next, the 1980s led to skyscrapers resisted by much of the counterculture and portending a further move toward banking and international finance but unfortunately accompanied by rising homelessness due to high housing prices.

And then another change with the development of the computer industry as the city and nearby San Jose became the United States center for the computer software business (centered here because of that "Junior" University, called Stanford) and what we call "high tech." The Bank of America and TransAmerica buildings have now been overshadowed by the SalesForce building, symbolizing the triumph of high-tech over banking and finance.

As a kid, I loved our family's day trips to San Francisco to see Stowe Lake in Golden Gate Park, the Cliff House along Pacific Highway, the old Sutros Baths, the Marina, the Presidio, the Golden Gate Bridge, and Marin County, Fort Mason, Fisherman's Warf, Twin Peaks, the Japanese Tea Gardens, Market Street, the buzz of the Business District, the impossible curves of Lombard Street, the incline of Jones Street (designed for horses, not cars, where the parked car wheels turn to the curb to avoid destruction), and the many prominent public museums.

San Francisco continues to maintain a rich diversity of neighborhoods, public parks, world-class museums, entertainment, nightlife, and restaurants. And, as a medical student, I explored most of them. I still love the city's sights and smells: the broad, green grass fields and trees of Golden Gate Park alongside delightful salted ocean air.

Common to life in big cities, you have a chance to rub elbows with famous people: for me, they have included Herb Cain, Diane Feinstein, Daryl Hannah, Jim Nabors, John Fell Stevenson, the Flood family, the Campbell family, the Scoma family, the Spreckels family, the Laird family, the Gonzalez family, Herb Boyer, William Henderson, Peggy Fleming, Patty Hearst, Jerry Mathers, Thomas Maneatis, and Cyril Magnin; some of us stay in touch.

My favorite San Francisco restaurants include, the Imperial Palace, Hunan House, Scoma's, Trader Vic's, and let me slip in Fentons in Oakland.

I love being a tour guide across the city.

Ah . . . those were the days.

So, as a newspaper editor used to say, "Go West, young man," and visit San Francisco.

My Favorite US Cities: Seattle

I HAVE HUNDREDS of relatives in the Seattle, Washington, area including Imbeau, Jacobsen (my mother's family), and Kilcup (my father's in-laws); at one time almost all the Kilcup relatives worked for the Boeing Company. Despite all these relatives, it remains one of my favorite United States cities.

Seattle is a beautiful city, built around a lake and up against the ocean with a huge harbor and channel to the sea, called Puget Sound, and Mount Rainer in the background. Along with San Jose and San Francisco, it has become one of our new high-tech cities with Microsoft and Amazon; it's also home to the famous Starbucks coffee shop chain.

I was only a baby on my first Seattle visit, to visit some of my father's family, but of course, then lived nearby in Portland, Oregon.

One of my most memorable trips was, at age 17, alone to visit both Kilcup and Jacobsen relatives; the trip included two days and a night fishing along the Sound to the Pacific Ocean; I learned more than I wanted to know about my Uncle Hugh and caught a great salmon, to boot. A Jacobsen uncle developed several successful small businesses in the area, and sadly, my brother and I last visited him just ten days before his death from melanoma.

The area of Seattle has been inhabited by indigenous peoples, the tribes of the Duwamish and Suquamish, for about ten thousand years. In more modern times, the city was named in 1852 for the contemporary Chief Seattle of the Duwamish, who favored good relations with the white man as long as they respected Indian land rights. Europeans first came in 1792, led

Seattle skyline

by George Vancouver on a British expedition to chart and map the Pacific Northwest.

Early business was logging, timber, and lumber; astonishingly, some trees loomed as high as four hundred feet and grew in rich stands; they are now long gone. Finished wood products were mostly shipped south to San Francisco. The "old days" were lawless and corrupt, mixed in with some skirmishes with the Indians; finally, the city grew enough to incorporate in 1865. But, because of corruption, the charter was canceled until reinstated in 1869. The Northern Pacific Railroad came in 1873, but to avoid Seattle's lawlessness and profiteering, terminated in nearby Tacoma, not coming to Seattle until 1884. Unionization and the Woman's Suffrage movement of the late 1880s began to "civilize" the town.

As in San Francisco, destruction and gold led to great change. The harbor and entire downtown were consumed by fire in June 1889. As in San Francisco, a banker, Jacob Furth, financed a rapid rebuild through his Puget Sound National Bank (later the Seattle National Bank). Furth came to San Francisco as a youth from Austria to become wealthy after the California Gold Rush, moving to Seattle in 1882 for "fresh air." Not only did he rebuild the city, but he also developed the water and electricity business, eventually financing the city's first synagogue. The Klondike Gold Rush of 1879 brought in a huge influx of prospectors and small business folks. The ambitions of this era lead to big changes in geology and culture: hills were removed, channels dug, sea walls constructed, and whole new residential neighborhoods built. The saying was "The miners mined the gold, and Seattle mined the miners"

The Space Needle

Pike Place Fish Market

Pike Place Fish Market

(from Wikipedia). By 1910, Seattle was a full-blown, mostly lawful, sophisticated city. It celebrated its rise to fortune with the Alaska-Yukon-Pacific Exposition of 1909.

Development during the era of the World Wars continued, but the city was almost destroyed by the Great Depression. It still depended mostly on the logging, timber, and lumber business, but during World War II it became a manufacturing center for ships and airplanes and their repair. Boeing Aircraft Company, founded by engineer William Boeing in 1916, became the region's largest employer and economic powerhouse (see "Airplane Travel Has Its Share of Ups and Downs"). It was said "as Boeing goes, so goes Seattle" (again, from Wikipedia). And Boeing often did swing between boom and bust, greatly affecting the Seattle economy. Ironically, one of Seattle's modern major tourist attractions, the Pike Place Market, arose from a Boeing bust after the Vietnam War. The Boeing headquarters are now in Chicago. South Carolina has a major Boeing manufacturing plant near Charleston.

The World's Fair of 1962, developed by Minora Yamasaki and Victor Steinbrueck, brought the world to Seattle's shores; the now-famous Space Needle observation tower and restaurant with surrounding plaza, remains from the Fair as an enduring tourist attraction and potent image of the modern Seattle.

High-tech now competes with Seattle's Boe-

ing economy. Bill Gates and Paul Allen returned home to Seattle from New Mexico in 1979 to build Microsoft. Biotechnology, food services, and retail have been added. Seattle still has less than one million people, contributing to its charm, but has all the culture, restaurants, and architectural amenities of much larger cities. My favorite Seattle restaurants include iconic, Canlis, Ray's Boathouse, Maximilien, The Nest, Zig Zag Café, and Matt's in the Market.

Some amusing stories:

- When visiting my dying uncle, he was surprisingly cheerful and eager to "go out;" I asked him where he wanted to go for dinner, on me, and he said, "Maximilien," so I took him and his whole family; he loved the evening but couldn't eat a bite (I probably

Chihuly Museum

Chihuly Museum

1962, when I was age 14, to attend the Century 21 Exposition; when we got there, my father unexpectedly said, "Well, here it is, let's go see my sister;" I couldn't believe it, so I convinced him to allow us at least four hours to walk around; moving fast, I managed to go through the United States Pavilion, the GE Exhibit, and any other free exhibit I could find.

- In the same plaza today stands an incredible museum dedicated to glassworks called Chihuly Garden and Glass; being a bit like my father, I guess, I told Shirley that I didn't want to go in to just look at a bunch of colored glass; boy, was I wrong; once in, she had trouble getting me out—it's marvelous.

could have flown to Hong Kong for the same price).

- My family drove eight hundred miles to the Seattle World's Fair in the summer of

While in Seattle, don't miss your own walking tour of the harbor and the old downtown; then take a cab up to the significant Woodland natural park, zoo, statuaries, and Japanese Gardens. A boat tour of Lake Washington is pleasant and allows you views of a part of the university, the iconic bridge, canals, and some famous homes including the walking path for Bill and Melinda Gate's guards.

Indeed, Go West Young Man, and when you do, don't overlook Seattle.

My Favorite US Cities: San Diego

San Diego skyline

MY PARENTS lived in El Cajon, a San Diego eastern suburb, for seventeen years, from 1982 to 1999, my father leaving retirement in Oakland to work in several of another Jacobsen uncle's businesses.

Uncle Rob moved to San Diego from Portland, Oregon, in 1968; he became successful in the computer software business, founding and then selling RJ Software. My father worked with him at a small manufacturer of water heat pumps called JEI Heat Pumps and then also with Uncle Rob's son at a computer printer repair and supply business called Lasers and Copiers. My father again retired, staying there, until moving to Stow, Ohio. But I had been going to San Diego for years, first for entry to Mexico, then to visit Uncle Rob, and then to visit my parents, bringing our children during Thanksgiving week; in addition, I visited for multiple medical conventions and business trips.

San Diego is a great city, snuggled along the coast between water and hill, temperate all year, and politically easygoing with moderate progressive local government. There is a sense of important business in the air, coupled with the enjoyment of life and the great outdoors despite a population of more than 1.5 million, all coexisting nicely alongside the obvious presence and importance of the US Navy and other military.

The indigenous peoples, the Kumeyaay, were touched by the Spanish first in 1542 by Juan Rodriquez Cabrillo sailing up from Mexico to claim Mission Bay for Spain, naming the area San Miguel. The site was later renamed by Sebastian Vizcaino in 1602, San Diego (Didacus) de Alcala, whose feast day was first celebrated there a few days later. In 1769, the Spanish brought multiple groups up from Mexico by land and by sea to establish an enduring colony. The famous Father Junipero Serra established the Mission San Diego the same year, growing it to 1,400 Indian Catholic priests thirty years later, and anchoring the El Camino Real leading northward to the

Franciscan Catholic Missions Father Serra founded all along the California coast.

San Diego remained part of California as it passed from Spanish to Mexican to American control. Its early existence was choppy, falling out of favor of state government due to poor finances, corruption, and faulty local decisions, losing its city charter from 1850 until 1889. But a move to the harbor and the arrival of the railroad in 1878 boosted its path to recovery, so that by 1915, it could host the Panama-California Exposition and in 1935 the California Pacific International Exposition, both enhancing the new Balboa Park. Curiously, the animals left over from the 1915 Fair were the basis of the San Diego Zoo, barely noticed then, but now world-famous. Balboa Park is now a major center for community, education, recreation, and just "being outside."

The military has been an important part of San Diego since 1850 when California formally became a US state. A Navy coaling station was built in 1902 at Point Loma with later developments of naval training centers, camps, hospitals, and air stations including the famous Miramar Air Station. The First World War brought aircraft manufacturing; Charles Lindbergh's plane, the "Spirit of St Louis," was built in San Diego by Ryan Airlines. The next war led to a huge expansion of both military installations and civilian populations; over twenty years, the population doubled to about 350,000 by 1955.

Post-war economic depression led the city to develop nonmilitary commerce. The economy expanded with shipbuilding, commercial

Balboa Park

and sports fishing, fish canning, electronics and high tech (particularly wireless communications), and most recently with a major rise of tourism featuring the deep-water military harbor and cruise ships, Coronado Island, Balboa Park and museums, Horton Plaza, the Gaslamp Quarter, a major convention center, Petco Park, the San Diego Zoo, the San Diego Zoo Safari Park, and SeaWorld. Downtown skyscrapers have made access to the downtown San Diego International Airport (Lindberg Field) difficult, but airport relocation has been blocked by widespread suburban development and geography. The city has an excellent education system, including the University of California with its colleges, medical school, and the Scripps Institute of Oceanography; there are many other state, local, and private institutions, giving the region a very high percentage of college graduates (45 percent). The Mexican influence is obvious and important. San Diego is an outdoor city and surrounded by many popular parks, preserves, and national or state forests all popular for hiking trails, camping, and exploration.

Ray and Joan Kroc moved to San Diego from the Chicago suburbs in 1976, two years after Ray purchased the San Diego Padres in a distress sale for only $12 million and to prevent the team from moving to Washington, DC. Ray Kroc was the successful founder of the McDonald's real estate and hamburger worldwide empire that sprang out of Kroc's discovery when he was a milkshake machine salesman, of a very successful hamburger stand in Bakersfield, California, owned by the McDonald brothers; the brothers eventually sold out to the new sales manager, and then moving back to the Chicago area, Kroc made important business history (see "The Hamburger," February 21, 2017, *Morning News-SCNow*). After Ray's death in 1984, Joan continued to have cultural and political influence in San Diego. She became part of the Gang of Four wealthy women (Joan Kroc, Helen Copley, Maureen O'Connor,

San Diego Harbor

and Susan Golding) that for a time had tremendous influence on the culture, development, and politics of the city, working together behind the scenes but also through public office and the newspapers they controlled. At Joan's death, she left the bulk of her estate to the local Salvation Army but also made her hometown in Minnesota happy with a $15 million gift.

My favorite San Diego restaurants include Chart House, Mister A's, Parma Cucina Italiana, The Mission, Eddie V's, Puesto, Monsoon Fine Cuisine of India, Casa Guadalajara, and The Taco Stand, and on Coronado: The Crown Room and Bluewater Boathouse.

Some amusing stories:

- In the old days, you could drive out to Cabrillo Point past Fort Rosecrans along dirt roads and watch the submarines come and go, and my uncle and I used to visit there, often in silence, but mainly to review our past year.
- My medical school roommate Bill and I went to visit my uncle and then on by train to Mexico City, or so we thought. Imagine Uncle Rob's surprise to hear me, only six hours later, call him from the bus station for a pickup; the Mexicans would not let us on the train, since we carried no cash but what they gave us back for the tickets.
- My son Charles and I went to the zoo one day—it's a huge place—and got separated;

despite my best efforts, I couldn't find him until assisted by the gracious Zoo Police.

- Once, when visiting my parents, who were then living in San Diego, I took them up to Disneyland; it was only their second trip to Disney and their first ride in a limousine; they were delighted.

- For a time, my Jacobsen grandparents also lived in San Diego, and I used to deliberately visit them in the morning to tease my grandmother on her tilt board.

- One reason I like Mister A's is that you can almost reach out from your dinner table to touch passing airplanes on airport approach.

When you go West, young man, make sure to include San Diego.

My Favorite US Cities: New Orleans

ALTHOUGH RELATIVELY SMALL at approximately half a million people (1.3 million in the metro area), New Orleans is a remarkable United States city, famous for its river and bayou life, food, music, culture, education, and a deceptive laissez-faire attitude.

I have been there more times than I can count as a tourist, conventioneer, and businessman. But believe it or not, I have never been to a Mardi Gras celebration. I have pre-viously written about one of its food inventions, the Poor Boy sandwich (see "Rich Boys Can Eat Po' Boys, Too," August 5, 2015, *Morning News-SCNow*).

When tormented by the British to leave Nova Scotia as Britain ethnically cleansed the French, forcing them in 1755 to flee (or be deported) to Quebec or Louisiana, or die, some of my Imbeau relatives moved south, although most moved to Chicoutimi, Quebec in Canada.

Bourbon Street

Doing some research in Pine Bluff, Arkansas, I found our family named in local records, Imbeaus moving north from New Orleans and eventually back again. Despite this heritage, I have never explored the Louisiana bayous; I need to.

Original indigenous peoples including the Chitimacha, the Natchez, the Chickasaw, and the Choctaw eventually were absorbed into the bloodlines of French, English, and Spanish settlers to form a people we now call the Cajun. The first major immigrating Europeans were the French in 1718, led by Jean Baptiste le Moyne de Bienville; then the Spanish took control after the Seven Years War in Europe. The Spanish delighted in helping the American rebels against Great Britain. The Spanish left behind enduring French Quarter architecture.

Control moved back to France in 1803. And then Napoleon, raising money to finance his European expansion, sold it all later in 1803 to those Americans, as part of the Louisiana Purchase, which was much larger than just modern Louisiana. Explosive growth followed, particularly after General Andrew Jackson's soldiers protected the city from English capture in the War of 1812. The French pirate and wealthy smuggler, Jean Lafitte, was pardoned by Jackson because of his assistance in this war.

By 1840, the city was the third-largest in the United States and its wealthiest because of mercantile trade, manufacturing, textiles, and the slave trade. Even by 1860, a majority of the people were mixed race, with the French language predominating. Over these years the African Americans also mixed in as the indigenous peoples before them, to be called Creoles, and became some of its wealthiest citizens, and on average more middle class than the rest of the United States. New Orleans black leadership and wealth continues to this day, although it has diminished.

After the United States Civil War, the victorious Union moved to ban the French language and culture and to limit Creole and Cajun influence. But at least the city was not badly damaged by war, except some Mississippi River levees and towns, although damage was suffered during the subsequent Reconstruction riots.

Along with postwar cultural changes, New Orleans also diminished as America developed Atlantic and Pacific ports, developed major east-west railroads, and then developed the automobile highways. America no longer needed the Port of New Orleans, the banks of New Orleans, or the business of New Orleans; other Americans also came to view New Orleans' important Cajun and Creole culture and peoples as arcane or eccentric. As trade and the economy declined, folks emigrated away from New Orleans, particularly the African Americans. By 1960, New Orleans had lost most of its cultural and economic status.

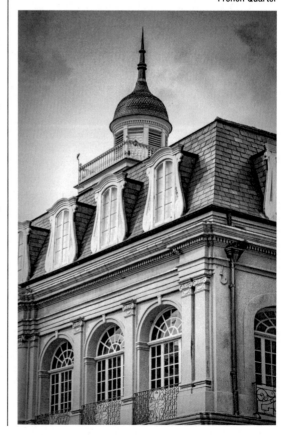

French Quarter

Then the city launched building projects with land reclamation and a serious turn to tourism. Tourism and trade became the cornerstones of New Orleans' new economy. The French Quarter was refurbished and expanded; new hotels were added, an impressive public River Walk built, restaurants rebuilt and added, and legal gambling brought to riverboats and a casino by Harrah's just off the French Quarter and the Ernest Morial Convention Center built alongside the Hilton Hotel. A trolley line linked the hotel district to the convention center and several city districts, including the Garden District and the Tulane University district. The Saints' Superdome (1975) was built alongside the Ninth Ward and later the World War II Museum (2000).

Hurricane Katrina struck on August 29, 2005. The city's levees were overwhelmed, and much of the city was destroyed. The New Orleans area witnessed an estimated 1,500 deaths, roughly $100 billion of damage, and the dislocation of approximately 50 percent of its population. Medical friends of mine, the Ellises, came to live in Charlotte for two years, and I gave them appropriate Carolina Panther NFL tickets so they could watch their beloved Saints. Rebuilding took at least six years, and even now, the Ninth Ward still needs some work. But the Saints were back for the fall 2006 NFL season.

I love to walk around New Orleans or drive along or across Lake Pontchartrain or drive along the coast to nearby Mississippi, or just take the trolley to all of its branches. And, of course, you must not ignore the French Quarter. I guess you should amble along Bourbon Street, ignoring the second-floor balconies, but also explore the French Quarter side streets. Go into the old antique and book shops, the art shops, the oyster bars, the piano bars, the old courthouse and United States Customs building, and the old churches. Even some of the old restaurants have historical and architectural value. Visit Preservation Hall Jazz center, Pat O'Brien's (to say you've been there), Jackson Square and shops, the modern shopping center whence stood the Jax Beer brewery, and finally, Café du Monde for some hot chocolate and beignets. You must spend at least an hour at du Monde, and if it's not yet midnight, walk along the river for an hour or so. You will love it all.

Other excursions deserve your time: the Garden District, the Tulane campus, the old Charity Hospital (now being redeveloped for Tulane University, housing, and shopping), and the Ninth Ward. Several famous surgeons trained at the old Charity Hospital.

Antoine's Restaurant

My favorite New Orleans restaurants include Antoine's, The Court of Two Sisters, Brennan's (actually, several of the Brennan Family restaurants), Arnaud's, K-Pauls, Galatoire's, Muriel's, Commander's Palace, Acme Oyster House, and Red Fish Grill. In addition to Preservation Hall, I have attended concerts by Benny Goodman and Al Hirt. I do not know the ghostly or Voodoo side of New Orleans aside from novels, particularly those by Anne Rice.

Some amusing stories:

• Slipping the floor managers at Preservation Hall one night an extra fifty dollars, we were able to sit for hours, but no drinks allowed—Shirley has a set of wooden statues of some Preservation Hall greats.

- I have yet to figure out how to manage the powdered sugar at Café du Monde.
- Once, in 1972, having lunch at Brennan's, in comes Vice President Agnew and entourage—the restaurant was emptied while he ate, but on return, our food was, of course, cold, so we got a new meal.
- I watched Canada defeat the 2010 US Olympic hockey team (I was "pulling" for the United States) on an amazing Sidney Crosby backward goal, through his own skates, on a TV set in a New Orleans hotel room.
- On a business trip, I was amazed when a table of musicians at Antoine's stood up to enthusiastically greet my friend; he was, in turn, surprised when several random couples came to greet me as we left the restaurant; I just winked at him.

Credit due: my introduction to an upstairs Antoine's waiter's family was by Ms. Rebecca of Florence, South Carolina—New Orleans born.

My Favorite US Cities: Chicago

Chicago skyline

CHICAGO IS the Midwest's largest city, probably always the most important, now the third-largest city in the United States. Its location on the southeastern shore of Lake Michigan is key to its history and success.

I was 17 when I first glimpsed Chicago. Eight years later, I moved to Madison, Wisconsin, for my residencies at the University of Wisconsin, so I was close enough to explore. My first date with Shirley was in Chicago in the summer of 1978.

Multiple trips followed, when I worked with the American Medical Association (AMA) as a resident recruiter, and now that I am involved in AMA and Allergy politics (the American College of Allergy is also headquartered nearby), I go about three times a year. Not to mention many other trips as a tourist, a conventioneer, and a businessman. I love the city.

The indigenous peoples—the Miami, the Sauk, and the Fox—were eventually organized into the Potawatomi tribes, whose word for garlic/onion fields ("shikaakwa") became the city's name. The first Europeans were the French; Jean Baptiste du Sable is known as the founder of Chicago, arriving about 1780. Indian lands were ceded to the United States after the War of 1812, and in 1833, most tribal peoples were sent to reservations west of the Mississippi River.

A town was organized in 1833 and incorporated as a city in 1837, growing quickly. At first, the economy depended on the water, stockyards, and railroads, but with population growth, manufacturing, retail, and finance became predominant. Commodities futures trading was first handled by the Chicago Board of Trade in 1848. Prosperity brought its Illinois politicians to national prominence, particularly Stephen Douglas and Abraham Lincoln. Lincoln became president of the United States. Ambitious public works projects in the late 1880s and 1890s—including a sophisticated sewage system, canals, and reversal of the Chicago River—allowed for significant growth.

Fire struck in 1871, destroying approximately four square miles of the city, possibly started by a downtown cow kicking over a lantern. But as in San Francisco and Seattle, the city grew back better than ever, this time with brick and steel construction. An American first, a steel-framed skyscraper, later copied in New York and around the world, came in 1885.

Immigration from all over the world catapulted Chicago to the fifth largest city in the world. The rise of organized public health systems also led to a significant public park system. Curiously, as a railroad hub, Chicagoans developed the North American time zones to serve the railroad schedules. The astonishing century was capped by the tremendous World's Columbia Exposition in 1893, probably the most influential world's fair ever, boasting more than 27 million visitors.

The World Wars brought more migrants, particularly from the Deep South, as manufacturing jobs rocketed. A rich African American culture arose in art, literature, and music; see the play *Jelly's Last Jam* (by George Wolfe, Susan Birkenhead, and Jackie Alexander, 1993) for some of this history.

Prohibition led to the rise in gangsterism, persisting, albeit somewhat more sophisticatedly, today; for a time, Al Capone was the richest man in America. The Great Depression devasted the city, since it was so dependent on manufacturing, with almost 50 percent unemployment. Labor unions became strong, and the Democratic party took over, never to retreat.

The next war rebuilt the city as its manufacturing might overtook the world, but the city was already rising from poverty, symbolized by the Merchandise Mart, completed in 1930; the mart was owned from 1945 to 1998 by the Kennedy family.

Chicago River

Renewed migration from the Deep South kept the factories humming. Its educational system, always strong, garnered everlasting fame for the University of Chicago, as there Enrico Fermi produced the world's first controlled nuclear reaction. The local construction projects included the Sears Tower (now Wells Tower), McCormick Place, and the O'Hare International Airport.

The politics remain Democratic controlled by the Irish and African Americans. The city's economy and culture remain strong.

Since 1905, the city has been famous for its public art, including building architecture, fountains, statues, parks, and public squares. Organized tours abound, but you can use walking maps. The river and lakefront have boat tours and boat rentals; the Chicago River spouts fountains of water each non-winter evening. Trips to Navy Pier, the Field Museum of Natural History, the Museum of Science and Industry, and the baseball parks (Wrigley Field and Comiskey Park—now Guaranteed Rate Park) are noteworthy.

I like walking along upper Lakeshore Drive (called the Gold Coast), through Millennium and Lincoln Parks, around McCormick Place, through the Trump Tower, and down Rush Street. Weekend walks along Michigan Avenue and State Street are a potpourri of art, craft goods, and hand foods.

My favorite Chicago restaurants include Delmonico's, Morton's, Chicago Chop House, Gibsons, Athenian Room, Riva, Volare, and Sapori Trattoria.

Some amusing stories:

- My first date with Shirley was late summer 1978 at Seven Dwarfs in Wheaton and, the next night, the Pump Room in Chicago. We got engaged about three months later.
- I often tell the drivers from O'Hare Airport how to navigate around traffic stops but also enjoy talking to them about their homeland politics or histories—some have

Aerial view of Chicago skyscrapers

also told me great Chicago stories and catch me up on local politics.

- I was in town the day after the Black Hawks won the Stanley Cup in 2010, the first time since 1961. The streets were jammed. I had to go underground and go through building basements to move around.
- Driving to O'Hare from Madison during New Year's season in 1978–79, I ran into one of their worst storms, forcing me to a hotel room for two days rather than a visit with Shirley. Despite the ice and snow, I tried to drive the highways, having three minor accidents, all in two days, but no real car damage, once missing a state trooper by inches on ice. I threw up my hands in apology; he gave me a "thumbs up."

Grant Park

- I frequently stay at the Chicago Hyatt Regency on Wacker Drive. Once the manager asked to meet me in his office, so I went down; the hotel had just finished some renovation, and he wanted to give me a tour. I laughed and said there was no need, but he anxiously insisted, saying he wanted me to give a good report, so I went. Afterward, he sent me a nice wine and cheese tray for my room, and I relayed the good news, I guess.
- One of my favorite Italian restaurants, Volare, is only about two blocks from the Hyatt, across the river, and I drag some of my friends there each June.

My Favorite US Cities: New York City

NEW YORK CITY is America's largest city with more than eight million people divided over five districts, called boroughs: Brooklyn, Queens, Manhattan, the Bronx, and Staten Island. My first visit was in 1972, and I have been there about thirty times since.

Believe it or not, New York started out as a Dutch territory.

Actually, the first Europeans were the French (1524) followed by the Spanish (1525), but the Dutch built the first lasting settlement in 1624, following on the work of Englishman Henry Hudson (1609), sailing for the Dutch East

Central Park

India Company. The Dutch bought Manhattan for sixty guilders ($1,000) from the indigenous Algonquin Nation (the local Lenape tribe).

The English finally did come and in 1774 established enduring English control after the Dutch-English wars, part of the Treaty of Westminster. The name was thus changed from New Amsterdam to New York, named for James Stuart, who was both the Duke of York and the English King James II.

The city became a trade and shipping center, employing a huge number of African-American slaves. In fact, by 1730, 42 percent of New Yorkers employed slaves, second only to Charleston, working on the docks and in the factories, not in homes.

The British made it a major base during the Revolution, once they had run off General George Washington's army. Much of the city was British Loyalist, thus also a haven for thousands of escaped slaves, later repatriated around the British Empire. After the war's end, it became the capital of the United States (first, the Confederation). President Washington was inaugurated on April 30, 1789, in New York, and most of the early Constitutional documents were written at Federal Hall along Wall Street.

The city saw tremendous growth in the next century, expanding to more than three million people. Slavery was abolished in 1827. Irish and German immigrants poured in to establish important business and political control, called Tammany Hall.

By 1860, half of the city was German or Irish. The Erie Canal completion in 1825 fed growth in commerce and finance, enabling business empires to move upriver to the Great Lakes, connecting the Atlantic Ocean to America's Midwest breadbasket and recently discovered oil.

With wealth came fine mansions, culture, arts, and literature. Great parks were built, including Central Park in 1857. But also, with rapid growth and wealth came social problems: civil unrest, worker riots, and factory decay. The Irish were in revolt but finally made peace with the Germans and English elites, leading to Irish control of the police department and ward politics.

A subway system in 1904 helped to heal the city and to bring all classes to mingle in Manhattan. A huge Southern Black migration in the early 1900s, fleeing the excesses of a post-Reconstruction South, brought racial balance and challenges to Irish supremacy, punctuated with the election of Fiorello La Guardia (Italian) in 1934 as a reformer.

The Brooklyn Bridge

Italian immigration was also huge in the first part of the twentieth century, with Italians making up 17 percent of the city by 1930. The Italians at first gathered according to their cities of origin but are now scattered all across the boroughs. Family, food, and religion held them together, and even today on Columbus Day, several feasts of St. Anthony and several feasts of Our Lady are well attended and highly venerated.

Italians from Sicily and Naples, in particular, organized groups to protect from each other and the Irish, with nicknames such as the Black Hand or the White Hand, later evolving into well-organized criminal families or gangs during Prohibition. Mob families remain important today, although like in Chicago, they are now more sophisticated and probably loosely organized across the country. Mayor La Guardia was able to curtail Tammany Hall and replace it with a "new" Democratic Party.

Asian immigration was also large. New York now far outstrips San Francisco with more than a million Asian origin inhabitants. Hispanic immigration also has changed the demographics of the City. The current city data is 33 percent non-Hispanic European (about half Jewish), 29 percent Hispanic, 26 percent Black, and 13 percent Asian. By 1940, New York was the biggest city in the Western world, outpacing London. A post-World War II housing boom continued to feed growth. Even so, Mexico City and many Asian cities are now larger.

Several movies and plays capture the evolving Irish, Italian, Jewish, Hispanic, Black, and Asian cultures, including *The Gangs of New York*, the *Godfather* trilogy, *West Side Story*, *The Jazz Singer*, *The Chosen*, *Harlem Nights*, *Jelly's Last Jam*, and several Jackie Chan movies, although movies mostly ignore the many positives.

Since 1930, New York has surpassed Chicago with high rises and skyscrapers. Much of the city's wealth has been driven by the ports and international finance. Fashion, publishing, accounting and legal, advertising, banking, media, insurance, retail, and real estate all have major national and international corporate headquarters in New York.

Wall Street has established international influence by pooling money from all over the world into American and international in-

New York City skyline

vestment. Wall Street and the idea of group investing in stock or bonds has enabled the building of America: our cities, our ports, our railroads, our real estate, our pleasures, and our businesses. This pooling of money allowed the rise of individual business and banking tycoons such as Cornelius Vanderbilt, J.P. Morgan, Charles Whitney, Jay Gould, Andrew Carnegie, Andrew Mellon, John D. Rockefeller, Henry Frick, Charles Schwab, Henry Ford, and others.

By now, you now know I like to explore cities by foot. That is only possible in New York neighborhood by neighborhood. Some neighborhoods I have never seen, but I have walked many. Your exploration can take you to Central Harlem—don't miss the Apollo Theatre and the world-famous Bone and Joint Hospital, along the East Side and the West Side, exploring both rivers—jogging, sort of, through Central Park with lakes, hills, playgrounds, and a marvelous carousel, along the harbor and Wall Street, through Soho and several other neighborhoods.

You can stop along the way at the great neighborhood restaurants for lunch or a snack. Explore the parks and many statues. Shop a little. Don't overlook Grand Central Terminal, the Empire State Building, or the Gracie Mansion. Visit the historic churches and synagogues. Spend some time at the Twin Towers Plaza and Memorial Museum.

Walk along Broadway, Madison Avenue, and Fifth Avenue, stopping at Rockefeller Center; ice skate in the winter or tour NBC studios or check out the new FAO Schwarz.

Many corporate headquarters have remarkable lobby art or plaza statues. Macy's is fun to explore, even if not shopping. Explore the Theater District and Times Square. Spend some time at the Lincoln Center; visit the Morgan Library, the Whitney Museum, and "The Frick" Art Museum. Visit the United Nations building. Visit the Statue of Liberty and Ellis Island. Save time for the American Museum of Natural History on the Upper West Side.

I have also explored the Brooklyn Promenade, Brooklyn Bridge Park, the Coney Island amusement park, and Brooklyn's Jewish neighborhoods and shops (but never on Saturday—although well-traveled, I seldom have elsewhere seen Hasidic fur hats, men only, called spodak or shtreimel). I have called the working folks of Queens my friends.

My favorite New York restaurants include Tavern on The Green, Café China, Mama Mia 44 SW, Katz's Delicatessen, The Russian Tea Room, Joe's Pizza, Oceana, The Carlyle, Del Frisco's Double Eagle Steakhouse, Benito One, La Nonna, Da Nico, The Palm Court, The Rose Club, Le Bernardin, and Colonie.

Indeed, few cities can match the "Big Apple." This nickname began in the 1920s, referring to the reward given to winning racehorses, formalized in the advertising logo search promoted by Mayor John Lindsay in 1971.

My Favorite US Cities: District of Columbia

The Washington Monument

I FIRST VISITED the District of Columbia in the summer of 1965 on a family trip to commemorate my high school graduation. We six spent approximately three weeks auto touring around the United States with three days in DC, staying with friends and relatives.

I will never forget it. DC has remained one of my favorite cities. I still am amazed by its activity, the huge government buildings, its parks, and its monuments. Now, many years later, I still am awed by the Lincoln Memorial, the Holocaust Museum, and the Vietnam War Memorial wall, as if standing on hallowed ground.

DC is a relatively young American city, founded in 1790 after the Revolutionary War with land donated by Maryland and Virginia along the Potomac River. Construction began in 1791. It was declared the new capital of the United States and named after General George Washington.

An important political agreement between New York and Virginia to locate the permanent US capital in Virginia territory was predicated on the central government paying for each state's respective war debt (the compromise of 1790). The ten-square-mile size of the district was set in the Constitution.

Washington's growth and development has always been fostered by its government role. All three branches of the US government have substantial presence, along with international groups, lobbying groups, and foreign governments. The British burned much of the capital in the War of 1812, but it was rebuilt, some reconstruction taking until 1868.

The district actually grew during the Civil War; President Lincoln was determined to continue construction on the Capitol building. By 1870, the city boasted 132,000 citizens but lacked amenities found in other large United States cities. Finally, modern infrastructure was wrought, including up-to-date plumbing by 1874.

President Franklin Roosevelt's administration, working to end the Great Depression, enabled huge building projects in the 1930s, including many of the buildings, monuments, statues, and parks we see today. The population surged past eight hundred thousand during World War II. The new visitors center under the Capital Building models this growth well.

The Lincoln Memorial

Since the 23rd Amendment to the US Constitution (1961), the district has been represented in the Electoral College, and since 1973, it has had its own mayor and city council. The district has one "at-large" representative in the US House of Representatives.

President Washington chose Pierre Charles L'Enfant to design and develop the city, and even though dismissed early, his name and credit remains. He envisioned radiating streets and board avenues with parks and walkways, with the Capitol building at the hub. His vision of a grand Avenue along the Mall was replaced by grass and water. Even though the skyline is dominated by the Capital and the Washington Monument, it's a myth that some law prescribed it so, but it is true that no building is higher than 555 feet. Pennsylvania Avenue connects the Capitol to the White House, Constitution Avenue, and Independence Avenue house many of the Smithsonian Museums and US agencies, K Street houses many lobbing and public relations companies and groups, and Massachusetts Avenue is the home of many foreign embassies.

Taxi cabs or newer for-hire cars are rela-

tively cheap for a national capital, but Washington is also very walkable. Similar to New Orleans, I have been to DC more times than I can count, but I still like to walk around; it's also fun to watch the famous people and admire the architecture. Start your tour slightly uphill at the Capitol complex visiting your senators and representative, tour the capital (ask your Congressional delegation for Gallery Passes), or at least go underground to the Visitor Center. Before going downhill, go behind the Capitol to the Library of Congress and the Supreme Court.

Then go back downhill past several statues, to the Smithsonian Museums. Most, but not all, of its buildings are along the Mall. I particularly like the Air and Space Museum, going by at least four times a year, as their exhibits are always changing. I also like their IMAX films. Along the way are several remarkable US Agency Buildings, including the FBI building, the Naval buildings, and the US Department of Health and Human Services building.

Near the Washington Monument is the awesome and emotional Holocaust Museum and the almost holy National Archives. If open and you are capable, climb to the top of the Washington Monument. Then take a detour north to the White House area and tour. Don't forget the other buildings in the White House complex and the striking Treasury building across the street.

The White House

The Capitol Building

Stroll past Ford's Theatre. Walk back to the Mall and the Reflecting Pool to move toward the Lincoln Memorial.

The Lincoln Memorial is the most revered building in the city. It was designed to inspire awe. Back to the Mall and past the Vietnam Memorial Wall, you'll see the new World War II Memorial and other important monuments as you move toward the Tidal Basin, the Jefferson Memorial, the Martin Luther King, Jr. Memorial, and the FDR Memorial.

In season, admire the magnificent flowering Japanese cherry trees (donated in 1912 by Tokyo). Move along the river through Rock-

way Parkway and up other hills to important neighborhoods, including Washington Square, Dupont Circle, National Cathedral Hill and the National Zoo area, Foggy Bottom with the US State Department, and Georgetown.

Georgetown could probably take a day of exploring by itself. Or take the Metro subway to all of these sites and more.

For a dramatic evening, take a car tour of the monuments alit; they are stunning. Other tours should include the Kennedy Center, the National Geographic Museum, the Arlington National Cemetery with the Curtis-Lee Mansion, and the Pentagon.

Extra time? Drive down to Mount Vernon or over to Andrews Air Force Base. Nearby Alexandria is also stunning.

My favorite DC restaurants include Nathan's, Oceanaire, Old Ebbitt Grill, Joe's Seafood, The Capital Grille, Bistro Bis, Karma, Masseria, St. Anselm, The Dubliner, Dumplings and Beyond, Tony Cheng's, and Founding Farmers.

If you love famous people sightings, go to Nathan's, Old Ebbitt Grill, Oceanaire, or The Capital Grille; you might even see me.

God bless America.

Arlington Cemetery

My Favorite US Cities: Charleston, South Carolina

Rainbow Row

BECAUSE I grew up in the West, I didn't know much about Charleston until moving to South Carolina in 1980.

Shirley and I first visited about three months after our arrival, encouraged by new-found Florence friends to attend Spoleto. We fell in love with the city at first sight; it remains one of my favorites. Indeed, it is, as the locals like to call it, The Holy City.

Charles Town was founded in 1670 by the eight Lord Protectors of English King Charles II, first governed by William Sayle, moving down to its current peninsular location in 1680–81. It became a major port and English cultural center and the oldest permanent English city in the American Colonies.

The Four Corners of the Law was established in 1680 at the intersection of Meeting and Broad streets, symbolic of the marriage of English Law and the Anglican Church—the Colonial Capital building on one corner and St. Philip's Anglican Church (now St. Michael's

Episcopal) on another. The city quickly grew with immigration from England, Massachusetts (Bostonians built winter homes in the area), Virginia, and the Caribbean bringing in other Protestant denominations: Congregational (1681), Baptist (1682), Presbyterian (akin to Congregational, 1731), and Methodist (1737).

It was wealthy enough by 1718 to attract the attention of Blackbeard, curiously demanding mostly medicines before sailing to North Carolina shores. By 1750, Charles Town was the wealthiest city in the colonies and by 1770 had become the largest Southern port.

In the late 1700s and early 1800s, more immigrants flowed in from all over Europe, contributing to growth and a religious melting pot. A major Jewish community has been established since at least 1762 and a Roman Catholic Church since 1791. Early slavery was based on indigenous people; by 1720, indigenous people made up 10 percent of the population.

Brought in later, African and Caribbean slaves established important Methodist churches since 1791, coming to be eventually called AME. Other important immigration into the upstate of South Carolina from the Atlantic colonies and Pennsylvania, mostly Irish or Scotts-Irish, eventually led to important political and cultural differences between the Upstate and the Charlestonians. The religious rigidity of the Charleston elite also led some Charleston Protestants to move "upriver" to settle in our Pee Dee region.

Charles Town launched into the American Revolutionary war in 1774 from the Four Corners Exchange Building. The English attacked in June 1776, expecting help from the Charles Town loyalists, but they were fiercely fought off by William Moultrie, the namesake for the fort from whence he forestalled the English navy, with the help of freshly cut wood and palmetto sand. Eventually, the English did capture the city, making it General Cornwallis' headquarters from 1780 to 1782.

Colonialists Francis Marion and Andrew Pickett carried out harassment raids against the English. The English were such ruthless and corrupt rulers that even their Charles Town supporters were glad to see them go. The city got rid of its British name (Charles Town) in 1783 and became thereafter Charleston.

The capital of the state was moved to Columbia after a suspicious fire at the Charleston Capital, the building becoming the Charleston County Court House. The invention of the cotton gin in 1793 turned the city into America's premier cotton port. The impact of the cotton gin also grew the city's black population so that by 1820 African Americans were the majority, but most were slaves.

Wealth also brought the idea of "states' rights" to Charleston so that by 1832 the whole state was ready to nullify certain federal laws or tariffs, drawing up formal documents of secession in 1852, though they were not executed.

The new US Customs House in 1849 was

Toward the Five Corners of the Law

testimony to the city's eminence. The majority party, the National Democrats, held its first meeting in Hibernian Hall in Charleston. In 1860, it met in Baltimore and was unable to nominate a consensus candidate. Thus, the Republican Abraham Lincoln became the new president of the United States, benefitting from a split Democratic vote between Stephen Douglas and John Breckinridge.

And then the American Civil War started.

Post-convention Charleston and Columbia secession agitation started in the fall, climaxing with a November torch and alcohol parade up Charleston's Meeting Street, including Georgians from nearby Savannah, streaming out from the famous Mills House Hotel. On Christmas Eve 1860, South Carolina ceded from the United States, and on January 9, 1861, Citadel cadets fired on the US Naval Ship the "Star of the West." President Abraham Lincoln was inaugurated on March 4. Fort Sumter was abandoned by the Americans in April.

Ironically, a fire, not the war, destroyed much of Charleston at the end of that year. A naval first, the Confederate States launched a successful submarine raid within Charleston Harbor against the USS Housatonic in early 1864, although the Hunley submarine crew all suffocated. The Union army occupied the city in 1865. The city's economy was shattered.

A huge earthquake in 1886 nearly destroyed the city again, damage calculated at about 25 percent of the city's dollar value. The city rebuilt and also organized politically to oppose United States Senator Ben Tillman, who was almost uniformly hated in Charleston since his governor days.

World War II continued the rebuild of Charleston as it became an important East Coast naval base and manufacturing site for war material and ships, similar to San Diego and San Francisco. In addition, unemployment was basically wiped out by the war. United States Congressman Lucius Mendel Rivers, chair of the House Armed Services Committee, encouraged further Charleston development by expanding Vietnam War-era United States military investment.

The aftermath of Hurricane Hugo (1989) and Mayor Joseph Riley (first elected 1975) changed everything and brought Charleston into its current ranking as an important modern United States city and a top United States destination for world travelers. Mayor Riley and Italian composer Gian Carlo Menotti brought Spoleto to Charleston in 1977 after several years of planning and failure, but that festival of concerts, plays, and other outdoor art, now successful with seventeen days in May and June, sparked a tremendous change in the city: a cultural change, a development change, and a mindset change.

Gazebo in Battery Park

Redevelopment, job development, enhancement of medical care, attention to education with a dazzling development of suburbs, colleges, infrastructure, arts, and restaurants are mostly due to Mayor Riley's success and the Spoleto "awakening." The festival brings people from all over, at least fifty thousand yearly, together spending approximately $40 million per year in the city.

I love to walk along the Battery to Battery Square and imagine myself a hero or villain in one of Pat Conroy's novels while looking out to Fort Sumter, or even taking a boat over to the National Park, walking through the quiet streets south of Broad lined with fine homes, strolling past the Four Corners of the Law, shopping in the Market Place (despite popular reputation, never a slave market), visiting the Charleston Place and shops, walking among the shops of Meeting Street or the restaurants of Bay Street, along the Waterfront Park harbor trail, or over to the new State Museum or aquarium, to the new docks and the huge cruise ships. In the old days, we used to be able to drive the streets of the nuclear submarine base. The final resting place of the Hunley submarine is now nearby.

Back downtown, take a carriage ride around the Historic District (the carriage guides are local college students who give a personalized version of local history, but maintain general truth) to view Rainbow Row, old and famous homes and mansions, including 1 Meeting Street, some with fascinating history.

Drive a bit and visit Middleton Place, the spectacular Ravenel Bridge, Mount Pleasant and Boone Hall, and the old Citadel—now an Embassy Suites Hotel on Marion Square with the nearby Holocaust Memorial and a statue of Dr. Leon Banov, Charleston's first Public Health physician, looking out to sea.

My favorite Charleston restaurants include Robert's (closed 2010 and now limited), SNOB, Maison, The Darling, Husk, 167 Raw, Charleston Grill, Peninsula Grill, 82 Queen, East Bay Meeting House, The Glass Onion, Stars, Halls Chophouse, and Great Wall.

And why The Holy City? It's complicated, but partly so named because of Charleston's large number of churches and synagogues; partly because of its long tradition of religious tolerance; but also, partly because it is so old and holds a hallowed place in South Carolina history, as the cultural, religious, and economic mother of the state.

APPENDIX

Morning News
Citizen Columnist Corps

TUCKER MITCHELL, Editor, *Morning News*

READERSHIP FOR NEWSPAPERS may be sagging just a bit.

But interest in being a newspaper columnist?

Not so much as it turns out.

Nearly forty *Morning News* readers took time to respond when we published an appeal two months ago, asking for "recruits" for our brand new "Citizen Columnist Corps." I was delighted with that response and pleasantly surprised at the diversity and skill of those who applied.

We've sifted through the candidates and come to a decision on ten "citizen columnists" who will write for us—and for you, of course—in the year ahead.

Each Wednesday we'll turn over our editorial page, most of it anyway, to our intrepid citizen columnists. We'll have two of them write each week, meaning you'll get to "meet" them all in about a month and then get to know them during the year ahead.

Their views, their choice of subject matter, and their personalities are unique. As one of the editors assisting with selections said after meeting our picks, they are "interesting."

Which is what we hoped they'd be.

Newspapers are, at their core, a form of entertainment. It's a specialized form, of course, one focusing on informing readers. But the truth is, if you are not entertained while being informed, you won't be back. There are other things to do.

So, we think the "Corps" will help entertain you. We also think it will give voice to some ideas and some perspectives not readily available through members of our staff or from the syndicated columnists who appear on our pages. Our crudely crafted (and not entirely serious) CCC motto—"Vox Populi Imprintins"—is supposed to mean something

Stephen Imbeau, Tom Sheehy, Jimmy Collins, Mary Gutman, Brice Elvington, Darlene Atkinson-Moran, Bob Stevens, and Jahn Hultgren, all members of the Citizen Columnist Corps, pose for a photo in front of the *Morning News* on April 4, 2013. Not pictured are Sara Mitchell and Teena Clarke.

—by Rebecca J. Drucker, *Morning News*

like "the voice of the people in print." What we mean by that is the voice of our readers in the newspaper.

Yes, we've had something like that for a long time through our Letters to the Editors section. And that's not going away. But here is something different.

It's an experiment, and it begins next Wednesday.

I'm excited to see how it turns out.

We asked members of the "Corps" to tell you a little bit about themselves. Their introductions are below.

Tucker Mitchell, Editor

About the Author

STEPHEN A. IMBEAU was born on November 25, 1947, on the wrong coast, in Portland, Oregon, growing up in Oakland, California. His parents were told to expect mental retardation since he was born with severe fetal distress, but they were pleasantly surprised when he met the childhood milestones, some even early. His father was a machinist for the Hyster Company, a subsidiary of the Caterpillar Company, and went on to become a salesman.

Imbeau grew up as a nerd, with absolutely no athletic ability at all, not dating until age 19, a junior in college. He attended college at the University of California at Berkeley in mathematics and computer science and then medical school at the University of California at San Francisco, graduating with a Doctor of Medicine degree in May of 1973. He completed both internship and residency in Internal medicine at the University of Wisconsin in 1977 and Allergy Fellowship in June 1979.

He married Shirley Ruth Burke of Toronto, Canada, in Toronto on August 18, 1979. In February, they left Wisconsin to come to Florence, arriving March 1, 1980, to three inches of snow, joining Dr. Peter Williams allergy practice. The first five years or so were tumultuous; after a few twists and turns, Imbeau began his own allergy practice in Florence as the first Board Certified Allergist in the region. The practice grew and grew and grew as he moved from independent practice to the Carolina Health Care Group to the Pee Dee Internal Medicine Group, and then with Dr. Joseph Moyer founded the Allergy, Asthma & Sinus Center in 1996.

In 1984, he became the president of the

Florence County Medical Society and joined the board of the South Carolina Medical Association in 1986, becoming its president in 1998. Early medical mentors in Florence included Drs. Frank Boysia, Hans Habemeir, Bill Hester, and Steve Ross; later Drs. Bruce White, Eddie Floyd, and Louis Wright also helped his medico-political career.

He got involved with the Florence Community first through the American Lung Association, the Big Brothers, the local medical review organization (PSRO), then the Florence Symphony, becoming president of the Symphony for six years, first in 1994. He joined the Chamber of Commerce Board and the Florence County Progress becoming chairman of County Progress in 1993. He became active in Mayor Frank Willis' campaign and worked closely with the mayor throughout his term and beyond.

He also developed a career at the American Medical Association (AMA), becoming alternate delegate to the AMA from South Carolina in 1996. He left South Carolina for a time to work at AMA with the American Academy of Allergy, Asthma, and Immunology, returning to the South Carolina Delegation at AMA in 2004. He became chair of the South Carolina Delegation in 2007 until 2015. In 2013, he became chairman of the Southeastern Delegation to AMA for two years; also, in 2011 he became Chair of the Elections Committee, and editor of the SED Newsletter in 2011, both offices continuing. He is also now the Chair of the American Medical Political Action Committee.

For more about Stephen and his writing, please visit *stephenaimbeau.com.*

Acknowledgments

ARTICLES REPRODUCED HERE with the permission of the *Morning News* and *SCNow*. I gratefully acknowledge the years of editorial assistance from Tucker Mitchell and Donald Kausler of the *Morning News* and *SCNow*. I also want to thank the many friends who have provided article ideas over the years. And finally, to my dear wife and noble traveling companions who have so graciously allowed and overlooked my eccentricities and adventures as I often wandered or even bolted away from the designated route, I love you all and thank you all very much.

My appreciation to the Credo House Publishers team: Tim Beals, Pete Ford, and Sharon VanLoozenoord. Well done.

PHOTO CREDITS

1. Wright Brothers' first flight, by John T. Daniels
2. Boeing logo, by Boeing Corporation, depositphotos
3. Airplane wing, by Sharon VanLoozenoord
4. Hamer Bay, by Shirley Imbeau
5. Muskoka cottage, by Shirley Imbeau
6. Muskoka view, by James Wheeler, Pixabay
7. Swiss train, by Stephen Imbeau
8. Germany Technology Museum, by Shirley Imbeau
9. Model trains, by Shirley Imbeau
10. Amtrak logo, by LeeSnider, depositphotos
11. '55 Chevy, by Barry Blackburn, Shutterstock.com
12. Stock cars, by Mybro, Pixabay
13. Old classic, by Sharon VanLoozenoord
14. Point du Hoc bunker, by merc67, depositphotos
15. Point du Hoc monument, by PTZ_Pictures, depositphotos
16. Hitchhiker, by Daxiao_Productions, depositphotos
17. Mount Tamalpais, by SvetlanaSF, depositphotos
18. CHP Patch, Wikipedia
19. St Andrews Golf Course, by brians101, depositphotos
20. Ducati motorcycle, by Sharon VanLoozenoord
21. Indian Motorcycle logo, by OceanProd, depositphotos
22. Glacier National Park, by Sharon VanLoozenoord
23. Harley Davidson logo, by chutimankuana, depositphotos
24. Beit Shean, by kaetana, depositphotos
25. Haifa panorama, by RnDmS, depositphotos
26. Map of Israel, by clinchuk, depositphotos
27. Star Legend, by Shirley Imbeau
28. Island Princess, by Sharon VanLoozenoord
29. Irish farm, by Shirley Imbeau
30. Harp logo, Republic of Ireland website
31. Guinness glass, by rohitseth, depositphotos
32. Berlin Wall, Niederkisrchnerstaße, December 1988, by Roland Arhelger, Wikipedia
33. New Berlin Wall exhibit, by Shirley Imbeau
34. Brandenburg Gate, by Shirley Imbeau

35. Jekyll Island Inn, by Judson McCranie, Wikipedia
36. Lord Coy Irvin, by Sidney Glass, the McLeod Health Collection
37. Brookgreen Gardens, by Sharon VanLoozenoord
38. Central Pacific logo, Wikipedia
39. Brookgreen Gardens statue, by Sharon VanLoozenoord
40. Hobcaw Barony, by Ben Theretoo, Trip Advisor
41. USS Arizona Memorial, US National Park Service
42. Pearl Harbor attack, Associated Press
43. British Parliament, by tommeaker26@gmail.com, depositphotos
44. Brexit protest, by Manuta, depositphotos
45. San Francisco skyline, by Shirley Imbeau
46. Lombard Street, by kwiktor, depositphotos
47. Golden Gate Bridge, by ventdusud, depositphotos
48. Cable car, by ventdusud, depositphotos
49. Seattle skyline, by pandionhiatus3, depositphotos
50. Space Needle, by jovannig, depositphotos
51. Pike Place Fish, by Shirley Imbeau
52. (b) Pike Place Fish, by blanscape, depositphotos
53. Chihuly Museum, by apinpomb@gmail.com, depositphotos
54. (b) Chihuly Museum, by Shirley Imbeau
55. San Diego skyline, by Steve Heap, depositphotos
56. Balboa Park, by flocutus, depositphotos
57. San Diego Harbor, by ViewApart, depositphotos
58. Bourbon Street, by sepavone, depositphotos
59. French Quarter, by Hambro, Pixabay
60. Antoine's Restaurant, Wikipedia
61. Chicago skyline, by dibrova, depositphotos
62. Chicago River, by Imel900, depositphotos
63. Chicago skyscrapers, by DesignOil, Pixabay
64. Grant Park, by Tess Wendorf, Pixabay
65. Central Park, by Maya Tanase, Pixabay
66. Brooklyn Bridge, by Free-Photos, Pixabay
67. New York skyline, by Frank Winkler, Pixabay
68. Washington Monument, by Steve Heap, depositphotos
69. Lincoln Memorial, by f11photo, depositphotos
70. White House, by lightscribe, depositphotos
71. The Capital, by Imel900, depositphotos
72. Arlington Cemetery, by Sharon VanLoozenoord
73. Rainbow Row, by sepavone, depositphotos
74. Charleston mansion, by Sharon VanLoozenoord
75. Toward the Four Corners of Law, by sepavone, depositphotos
76. Battery Park, by Sharon VanLoozenoord